OVER-RULED ON WELFARE

The increasing desire for choice in education and medicine and its frustration by 'representative' government

RALPH HARRIS ● **ARTHUR SELDON**

The report of a 15-year investigation into private preferences and public policy based on surveys in 1963, 1965, 1970, 1978 into priced choice between state and private services

Paperback : xxx+249 pp. With 6 Appendices, 10 Charts and 43 Tables

Price: £3·00   ISBN 0-255 36122-X

Published *in* June 1979 by

Hobart Paperback No. 13

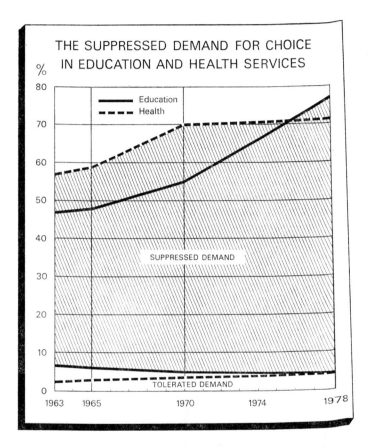

THE SUPPRESSED DEMAND FOR CHOICE IN EDUCATION AND HEALTH SERVICES

%

— Education
▬ ▬ Health

SUPPRESSED DEMAND

TOLERATED DEMAND

1963 1965 1970 1974 1978

The lower line for education represents the number of children in private schools as a proportion of the total of children of school age; the lower line for health represents the number of people privately insured for medical services as a proportion of the total population (the percentages are shown in the panel on 'The Potential Market for Education with Choice', Ch. 5, p. 89). The upper lines show the percentage of people in the 1978 sample who favoured the two methods of opting out of education and the NHS (Tables II and IV, Ch. 3). The lower lines broadly indicate the amount of private provision in education and health allowed by the state, and the upper lines indicate the suppressed desire for private education and health services.

OVER-RULED
ON WELFARE

The increasing desire for choice
in education and medicine
and its frustration by 'representative' government

A 15-year investigation
into private preferences and public policy
based on surveys in 1963, 1965, 1970, 1978
into priced *choice between state and private services*

Ralph HARRIS • Arthur SELDON

Published by
THE INSTITUTE OF ECONOMIC AFFAIRS
1979

WA

First published in 1979 by
THE INSTITUTE OF ECONOMIC AFFAIRS
2 Lord North Street, London SW1P 3LB

© The Institute of Economic Affairs 1979

Printed in England by
Goron Pro-Print Co. Ltd., Lancing, West Sussex
Text set in Monotype Times Roman 11 on 12pt.

Contents

TABLES
Introduction

Chapter 2

Chapter 3

Introduction

Readers new to the *Choice in Welfare* surveys are owed an explanation of their origin, objects, method, and the reliability of the results.

The origin and objects are outlined in Chapter I.

METHOD

The method has been to combine market research and opinion polling in an effort to discover preferences in the large part of the purchases made for the British individual (or family) by other people over whom he (or it) has no direct, day-to-day control.

Over the roughly half of earnings—'take-home-pay' —left after taxes (including rates and social insurance) the earner has direct day-to-day control by spending it in the market and exploiting the choices it offers between competing suppliers. The market, like all human institutions, is always imperfect, and its various sources of 'imperfection' have been studied assiduously for 200 years in a vast economic literature on the diagnosis of causes and the prescription of cures. But for the other half of earnings spent by government and officials in the political market, the individual or family has no direct, day-to-day control, or even influence. Government does not know how earners would like their taxes spent, whether they are content with the ways in which it is spent, and whether they would like reforms. The earner's control through 'representatives' in Parliament and local Councils is remote, indirect, infrequent, spasmodic and weak. Nor does government wish to know. It would rather be left to its own devices. And the recent efforts to introduce the voice of the parent-earner in *ad hoc* machinery like Parent-Teacher Associations or area health authorities remains defective because they too rest on 'representation' that cannot speak effectively for all the earners whose earnings the representatives or, even worse, permanent officials are spending.

For some of the goods and services supplied by government this unsatisfactory machinery of indirect representation is unavoidable because no other method is practicable for such collective activities as national defence or local preventive medicine. But for most—possibly two-thirds—of government supplies, this is not true, because they can be bought and sold in competitive markets. This is largely the province of 'welfare', mainly education and medicine, the two massive services in kind that government supplies 'free'—in return for compulsory payments called taxes. Here direct personal control is practicable but prevented by the intellectual error of academics, by the confusion of demagogues and by the vested interests of politicians, bureaucrats and trade unionists in national and local government.

Since no post-war government has moved to discover preferences and create earner-control in these unnecessarily state-controlled services, we have tried to provide the only possible substitute. We set out in 1963 to discover public opinion on how individuals would like their welfare services supplied and whether they would prefer to pay for them indirectly through taxes or directly by fees and charges eased by insurance.

TWO CENTRAL INQUIRIES

We have now completed four surveys: in 1963, 1965, 1970 and 1978. (The 1978 questionnaires and cross-sections of the population are detailed in Appendices A, B, and C.) We have used two methods. *First,* to discover broad national preferences between government and private suppliers in education and medicine, we have asked questions on three alternative national ('macro') policies: paying more in taxes for more or better state welfare; leaving the state services to cater for people in need but arranging for the people in general who can pay to contract out, take their money and obtain welfare where they prefer; or leaving the state services to provide for everyone but allowing individuals who so prefer to contract out. *Second,* to discover what each earner would prefer, we have asked questions on whether he/she would prefer as ('micro') individuals to continue as now or accept a refund of taxes in the form of vouchers for schools and health services and add to them to pay fees for private education or health insurance premiums for medical consultation and treatment.

In both kinds of inquiry we have gone as far as possible to emphasise that the alternatives would have to be chosen in the knowledge of their costs. The macro-questions have indicated that taxes were a method of payment for state services, and that if other services were preferred they would have to be paid for in other ways. And the micro-questions have stated in figures the costs or prices of private education and private health insurance.

Throughout the four surveys we have centred the inquiries on these two kinds of information about preferences between state and market. All the other questions have been secondary or subsidiary. They have been intended to discover how much people know of the costs or prices of state and private education and medicine and have made certain that individuals in the sample knew the approximate or estimated real figures before being asked their choices.

POSSIBILITY OF ERROR IN NEW TERRITORY

We were aware that we were entering new territory, that most people had never been asked such questions, that they might have difficulty in understanding them, that family decisions were in practice often made after much reflection between husbands and wives, that the results would have to be treated with reserve, or even extreme scepticism. It was often difficult to phrase questions in a manner that would make their meaning unmistakable to people—some 95% of the whole sample—who had no reason to know state costs or private prices, who had never made such decisions, and who without much preparation might not have grasped fully the choices they were expressing. The degree of knowledge and understanding may differ between men and women, younger and older people, lower- and higher-income groups. Such uncertainties made us doubt the findings of the first survey in 1963 until a second survey in 1965, a third in 1970 and the fourth in 1978 strongly confirmed both the existence of unexpressed preferences that were unheard in the making of public policy and the fluctuating but clearly upward general trend in the desire for a choice outside the state.

It is because of the unavoidable possibility of error in the details of the field surveys that confidence in the broad orders of magnitude could be built up as the trend was displayed over two years (to 1965), seven years (to 1970), and then 15 years (to 1978). We have made the present report an historical review of all four surveys as far as repetition of questions makes possible. Refinements in the questions, the addition of a full complement of women in 1978, and differences in the degree of detail in the analyses of the results have confined the 15-year narrative to the main features. But these are where the possible errors and imperfections are least, and where the findings are most reliable.

NEW INQUIRY IN 1978

In the fourth survey we repeated the main macro- and micro-questions to maintain the historical continuity but also added a new series of questions to discover how much people know of where their taxes are being spent, whether they are content, or whether they wish for redistribution of tax revenue, for addition by higher taxes, or for diminution by return of taxes. These answers would give an approximate impression of the extent to which taxes were being spent in accordance with the wishes of taxpayers, and therefore test the claim made for parliamentary government that it is representative. The questions were especially difficult to formulate; and the very difficulty is a reflection on the state of public knowledge, or lack of knowledge, and of the destruction of information in a 'price-less' system in which education and medicine are supplied substantially 'free'. We have been reticent in reading conclusions into the details for small sub-groups, but the main results seem incontrovertible.

In view of the interest in public attitudes to taxation focussed by the June 1978 vote in California on Proposition 13, with its two-to-one approval for tax limitation, we tried to frame questions to elicit replies that would constitute a first approximation to a 'Proposition 13, GB'. Here, too, despite teething troubles, the main results seem valid and important (Chapter 2), especially since the questions were tried in two variations on two samples by two market research/opinion polling specialists. (Percentages do not always add to 100 because of computer rounding to whole numbers.)

CONVERSION: SAMPLE POLL TO NATIONAL TOTALS

The data emerges from the survey in the form of the number of people in the sample and each sub-group who answer the questions, the number giving the various possible replies, and the percentage of the latter to the former. For example, of the total sample of 1,992, representing all working men and women aged 16 up to 65, 70% in answer to Question 4a (Questionnaire: Appendix A) said they would wish their taxes spent differently from the ways in which it was now spent by government. And there were small differences between men and women and the two occupational groups, though little between younger and older people, between Labour and Conservative sympathisers, or between people with less (or shorter) education up to 16 and those with more (or longer) education over 16.

The basic statistics have been used to derive three

more kinds of information. First, the main percentages have been converted into numbers of people (Table I). Thus since the 1,992 sample represents 21 million full-time working people[1] aged 16 up to 65, 70% of the total who wanted their taxes spent differently is converted to

Table I
Sample and Sub-Group Bases and Conversions to Population Estimates

Sample/ Sub-group	Base	Approximate Working Population (to nearest million)
Total	1,992	21
Men	1,142	12
Women	850	9
Age: 16-34	825	9
35-64	1,164	12
Occupational: ABC1	782	8
C2DE	1,208	13
Political sympathy: Con.	673	7
Lab.	537	6
Others, 'don't know', etc.	782	8
Education: up to 16	1,568	17
over 16	398	4

15 million. And all these figures are put into Table I to show the relative sizes of the sub-groups.

PERCENTAGES OF SAMPLE TO VOTES IN 'VOTES CAST'

In most questions people were invited to reply with definite answers or say 'don't know'. In many the

[1] Defined as working at least 30 hours per week.

'don't knows' are up to 10%. In others people were invited to 'guess' the replies and many were far out. This is not a criticism of the sample: the extent of the 'don't knows' can be a valuable indicator of the extent of public knowledge or lack of knowledge. Nor is it a criticism of the survey or of the questionnaire: the IEA surveys have asked questions never put to the public, and it was to be expected that some would not feel confident to give a definite reply, or that others would reply (or 'guess') wrongly.

In the meantime, since these questions are not asked by government, the IEA surveys are the only available substitute. Though a 'second best' because based on a sample and not on the whole electorate, they are nevertheless the best 'second best' available, and are thus the first indication of what a national vote or referendum on these issues would be. For this purpose we have recalculated some percentages by omitting the 'don't knows' and showing percentages of 'votes' cast. Thus for the 'votes' on limiting taxes the 'don't knows' were numerous and there were also some who 'would not say'. 57% were for a limit, 15% against, and 27% were neither. If the figures are recalculated as percentages of the 'votes' cast one way or the other, they become 79% for, 21% against.

PROJECTION

The four surveys cover the period 1963 to 1978. Even though they indicate trends rather than spasmodic movements without any general direction, it is impossible to say whether the trend will continue unchanged, accelerate or decelerate. But public policy decided now will last years or decades before it can be changed, and the better the information on which it is based the less likely it is to be damaging or wasteful. There is no reason to suppose it is necessarily misleading to consider where the trend may be in, say, 5 or 10 years—in 1984 or 1989 or even beyond. We therefore indicate how the trend in several basic preferences, both micro and macro, may develop in the 1980s. They are shown in Tables and Charts in Chapters 3 and 5. We emphasise they are projections of past trends on varying assumptions, not forecasts or prophecies. We are not arguing what the preferences will have become by 1984 or 1989, but where they will have reached if the trend of the past 15 years continues in one or more possible ways, which it may not.

RECEPTION BY INTERVIEWERS AND
RESPONDENTS

Not the least indication of the authenticity and value of the responses to the inquiries is the reaction from the trained interviewers and the co-operation of unprepared people in the sample, who, we may recall, were in both sexes, all ages from 16 to 65, in all socio-economic groups and with all political party sympathies (or none).

The three earlier studies were highly popular with interviewers from start to finish because they found the questionnaire was interesting and respondent co-operation was high. Last-minute addition of the local government questions in 1978 gave interviewers a hard day's work; and the 'arithmetical' questions were 'a real problem' to the less numerate among them. But

after the interviews were completed, respondents' comments indicated varying responses, and interviewers
reported the following reactions:

- Respondents were quite willing to help with the
  survey. The general feeling was one of interest in
  knowing how their money was spent.
- This survey did not seem as 'flippant' as some others
  . . . even though the respondents might have been
  slightly taken aback and had to give some thought
  to the questions. Some felt slightly flattered that their
  opinion was being asked about such important
  matters.
- Most of the people interviewed went ahead 'with
  gusto' when they saw what it was about . . . 'I found
  nobody bored at all'. The main reaction was 'Will
  this survey help us by putting our views so that something will be done?' (This in a sense seems to us the
  most significant reaction of all.)
- 'I took along a plain notebook so that the respondents
  could work out their figures. They all did it very
  painstakingly with much crossing out. They all found
  it very interesting and I had a job to get out, as they
  wished to discuss it further after I had finished.'
- Informants seemed to get 'quite interested', particularly after they had split the money up on seeing the
  correct percentages. The majority 'really seemed to
  be intelligently interested'.
- There was considerable interest in the rural areas.
  People were 'intrigued that they could have a say in
  how taxpayers' money was spent'.
- Men were most interested but 'the women tried to
  get away'.

- 'This is a well-remembered survey, chiefly because it required much more thought from the members of the public. About 80% of my respondents were very interested and concerned, and went to much trouble to give their considered opinion.'
- 'This survey created a great deal of interest, although it was difficult to get across to the public. Once interest was there, however, it was held to the last question.'

This enthusiasm was not universally found by interviewers; about a quarter of interviewers who submitted comments remembered the survey 'with distaste', almost always because it was 'difficult' or 'too remote from everyday life'.

Another interviewer said:

- 'Although most respondents completed the questions, from the comments passed on not all of them understood it.'

The view that respondents were sceptical was also expressed by another interviewer, but here the argument was that far *longer* should have been spent, so that people could ponder the questions and work out the answers in more detail. The scepticism was less against the subject matter than against the method of approach, which some respondents thought 'too superficial for such a complex subject'.

These are minority views. Generally the survey was widely seen as popular among respondents, if far less so among interviewers.

Clearly the questions were found difficult by some respondents, and allowance for misunderstanding in the replies must be made in interpreting the results. But 'difficulty' must be understood in the sense of unfamiliarity. There was little in the 'arithmetic' that was inherently beyond the capacity or even daily experience of the sample as a whole. And, to the extent that some questions were beyond some respondents, there is here a reflection of the failure of the state to inform its citizens of affairs with which they should have some acquaintance if they are to make responsible judgements and choices in electing Members of Parliament to take the decisions for them. Not least, where the information is commonly available, as it is in the market for everyday or household purchases, ordinary people can learn to make responsible choices—which are, moreover, better informed in the light of their family circumstances that they must be presumed to know better than officials or politicians.

OUTLINE OF THE REPORT

Our 1978 report opens with an account of the original thinking that led to the first survey in 1963. Chapter 1 recounts the reaction to early IEA reports that led to the realisation that the unproven objection of 'politically impossible' had to be investigated and rebutted if potentially fruitful lines of inquiry were not to be still-born.

Chapter 2 opens the report on the findings by reviewing the effort to construct a short parallel to the California Proposition 13 on tax limitation to indicate the general mood of public attitudes to British taxation in 1978.

Chapter 3 explains the application of 'political market research' to welfare in the first of the two main lines of inquiry: the 'macro'-economic questions on three national options in welfare policy.

Chapter 4 discusses the comparative efficiency of the ballot-box and the market in meeting consumer preferences, and sets the stage for the second main line of research in Chapter 5—the micro-economic questions based on the idea of topping-up education and health vouchers, in order to discover the strength of the demand for a choice in education and medicine.

Chapter 6 reviews the effort to discover how the British would like their taxes spent and how far British representative government is representative.

Chapter 7 analyses the latest government statistics (for 1977) on the taxes that the British people have been paying and the social benefits they have been receiving in return, as a background to Chapter 8 which discusses proposals for policy in the light of the research findings.

We should add that, although we have received advice from many quarters, both sympathetic and hostile, we take full responsibility for the methods we have built into these studies, not least the rigorous systematic introduction of price wherever possible and as precisely as possible, and for the interpretation of the results. Although our judgement or opinion may not be shared by advocates of the Welfare State, presumably no-one will quarrel with the data assembled by the scrupulous attention, above all by Mr England, to the accepted principles and methods of scientific sampling, interviewing and computer analysis. Responsibility for the method and the interpretation of the findings remains with us.

RALPH HARRIS
ARTHUR SELDON

March 1979

The Authors

RALPH HARRIS was born in 1924 and educated at Tottenham Grammar School and Queens' College, Cambridge. He was Lecturer in Political Economy at St. Andrews University, 1949-56, and has been General Director of the Institute of Economic Affairs since 1957. He wrote (with Arthur Seldon) *Hire Purchase in a Free Society, Advertising in a Free Society, Choice in Welfare,* etc., for the IEA. His essay, 'In Place of Incomes Policy", was published in *Catch '76 . . .?* (Occasional Paper "Special" (No. 47), 1976). His most recent works, written with Arthur Seldon, are *Pricing or Taxing?* (Hobart Paper No. 71, 1976) and *Not from Benevolence . . .* (Hobart Paperback No. 10, 1977); and he contributed the Epilogue, 'Can Confrontation be Avoided?', to *The Coming Confrontation* (Hobart Paperback No. 12, 1978).

Mr Harris is Secretary of the Wincott Foundation and the Political Economy Club, formerly secretary, now a Vice-President, of the Mont Pelerin Society, and a Council Member of the University College at Buckingham. Mr Harris lectures and writes widely on post-war policies and the economic requirements of a free society.

ARTHUR SELDON was born in London in 1916, educated at Raine's Foundation School and graduated from the

London School of Economics. He was a Tutor in Economics for the London University Commerce Degree Bureau, 1946-56, and a Staff Examiner in Economics to the University, 1956-66.

After editing a retail journal and advising in the brewing industry, he joined the Institute and wrote its first *Paper* in 1957 (on pensions), its early reports on advertising, hire purchase and welfare with Ralph Harris, and several later *Papers*. He is co-author (with Ralph Harris) of *Pricing or Taxing?* and *Not from Benevolence . . .*; and he contributed the Prologue, 'Change by Degree or by Convulsion', to *The Coming Confrontation*.

He wrote *The Great Pensions Swindle* (Tom Stacey, 1970), and compiled *Everyman's Dictionary of Economics* with the late F. G. Pennance (J. M. Dent, Second Edition 1976). He wrote *Charge* for Maurice Temple Smith, 1977. He contributed an essay, 'Individual Liberty, Public Goods and Representative Democracy', to the Hayek Festschrift, *ORDO*, 1979. He has been a contributor to the *Economist,* the *Financial Times, The Times* and the *Daily Telegraph.*

Acknowledgements

to our advisers, assistants and the 10,000 who have answered our unprecedented questions

Since this is the last of four reports, in which we assemble the main findings in an historical and analytical review, we wish to thank all those who have advised, cautioned and encouraged us in applying a unique amalgam of known techniques of commercial market research and political opinion polling, with an admixture of original ingredients, to new subjects of inquiry.

Since much of the fourth survey in 1978 was based on the experience acquired in the first three, we would thank the following economists and market research specialists whom we consulted on the early inquiries:

Economists
Dr Colin Clark
Dr Michael Canes
Professor Dennis Lees
Professor A. T. Peacock
Professor A. R. Prest
Professor A. A. Shenfield
Professor E. G. West
John B. Wood

Market research specialists
Dr Mark Abrams
Mr John Downham
Dr R. P. Kelvin
Dr J. A. P. Treasure

We also thank Professor Charles K. Rowley, co-author of *Welfare Economics: A Liberal Re-statement,* for discussion on the social welfare function (Note to Chapter 6).

Above all we thank Mr Leonard England, originally

of Mass-Observation and later of England, Grosse & Associates, for his technical advice—and exertions— over 15 years since the first survey, and Miss Wendy Grosse, his colleague. Mr John Davis provided the 1978 note on margins of error (Appendix D).

Among IEA staff we thank above all Michael Solly for dedicated and scrupulous work on all four surveys ranging from research and scrutiny of the text and statistics to supervision of the material through the press. We also thank Hamish Gray for his work on the 1970 report, Robert Miller for research and editorial assistance on the 1978 report, Kenneth Smith for prompt discovery of elusive sources for the 1970 and 1978 surveys. Not least we are indebted to Joan Roffey for good-tempered re-typing of successive drafts, and remarkable accuracy in deciphering partly illegible longhand.

Goron Pro-Print have served unconventional authors and perfectionist proof revisers with outstanding accuracy, promptitude and patience.

RALPH HARRIS
May 1979   ARTHUR SELDON

Prologue

The Past: The Welfare State

The British Welfare State removes the essential requirement for rational choice by concealing from citizens information about the cost of its numerous services, in particular education and medical care. In so doing it is trapped in a dilemma that may prove its downfall. For to maintain the claim that the very purpose of the Welfare State is the separation of payment from consumption by supplying services 'free', it must make a virtue of necessity by claiming that ignorance is better than knowledge, that neglect of cost is better than awareness of cost, and that obscuring the link between price and benefit will have no effect on the volume or efficiency of the resources used in services it emphasises as especially indispensable for tolerable life or civilised living.

Having made it impossible for the public to compare cost and satisfaction (or dissatisfaction) in services consuming a quarter of the national income, politicians of all parties make no effort to assess how far their 'customers' would prefer resources shifted from one use in welfare to another, or to pay more in taxes for better state welfare, or pay less in taxes and pay privately for services of their choice. There is no informed discussion of adjustment of expenditure on state services 'at the margin', which is the common

1

spontaneous outcome of the ceaseless search for improved production and consumption in competitive markets where the individual is spending his own money. Nor have the evident shortcomings of the collectivist method in welfare prompted an open debate on alternative policies that could achieve its proclaimed, but unrealised, purposes without mounting bureaucracy, soaring taxation, contempt for individual preferences, declining standards, financial strain and periodic convulsions, as at the start of 1979, in state (but not private) schools and hospitals.

Instead, to the obfuscation of the financial implications of state welfare, politicians and their academic advisers have added confusion to such debate as independent scholars have endeavoured to open up. By the standards of post-war discussion, anyone who questions the method of the British Welfare State is assumed to be calling in question its aims and therefore to be lacking in concern, caring, conscience, 'compassion'. That ready rebuke has been enough to silence many who might otherwise have expressed in public the doubts they could not stifle in private.

At the Institute of Economic Affairs, a number of economists who were not interested in political fictions, nor dependent on public (=political) sources of finance,[1] persisted with their researches and analysis. The early results were encouraging (Chapter 1 and Appendix F).

International scholars, especially in the United States, began to illuminate the public debate, particularly by studying the self-serving motives that lead politicians

[1] The IEA does not accept government finance, directly or indirectly.

and bureaucrats to advocate policies which do not—
and are not intended to—serve any convincing interpretation of the 'public interest'. Little wonder political
party men have shown no interest in trying to discover
whether those they claim to represent would prefer
alternative policies.

If unreflecting support for the British Welfare State
was founded on nothing more substantial than ignorance of cost and unawareness of alternatives, it seemed
to us worth at least one more effort, the fourth since
1963, to shed light for the benefit of a wider audience
than is reached by more specialist IEA studies. In addition to presenting new material from the 1978 survey,
we have therefore summarised argument that continues
to be neglected. Our aim is principally to dispel
prejudice by combatting the ignorance and incompre-
hension on which prejudice—along with the present
Welfare State—has rested for too long.

CHAPTER 1

Genesis: The Myth of 'Politically Impossible'

The Institute set out in 1957 to re-investigate the market as a device for registering individual preferences and allocating resources to satisfy them. These are the twin essential purposes of an economic system wherever scarcity enforces choice, economy and sacrifice, in 'welfare' as well as in every other productive human action.

The market had been increasingly neglected by politicians, economists and sociologists since the 1870s. 19th-century Fabian teaching was that government, local and national, was superior to 'capitalism' for organising resources to serve human requirements. Pre-war Keynesian teaching was that government could avoid the fluctuations of booms and slumps by 'managing' demand. And war-time Beveridge teaching was that only the state could ensure freedom from the five 'giant evils' of Want, Disease, Squalor, Ignorance and Idleness (his capitals).

No doubt this teaching was mis-used by followers of all three schools of thought to pursue objectives that would not have been approved by the more liberal-minded Fabians, by the liberal Keynes, or by the liberal Beveridge. Yet Fabian teaching has been used to hobble and almost destroy the developing market in national government transport, fuel, health, pensions, etc., and local government education, housing, refuse collection, fire services, etc., none of which has to be supplied by political bureaucracies. Keynesian teaching has been used to extend the control of the state from budgeting for government to budgeting for the nation as a whole, and to tighten its control over banking and finance, and even industry and commerce. And Beveridge's teaching has been used, not least by the Titmuss school of social administrators, to extend the power of national politicians and local officials over the intimate personal lives of the people in health, housing, pensions, education, and in many other ways.

In 1957 it seemed to some of us that the case against the market had been accepted uncritically and that the case for replacing it by government was a *non sequitur*.

The market is a network of inter-connections between people coming together as buyers and sellers, in everyday requirements or in welfare. The market is imperfect, but it does not follow that government would make a better job of matching supply to demand by being more efficient, more sensitive to individual requirements, more equitable, or even more democratic. It has imperfections that arise from the nature of the political machinery it has to use. To argue that the market should be replaced by government requires the advocate to show that the imperfections of government are less objectionable than the imperfections of the market. That he has not done; and there is a growing body of economic thought which argues that he cannot do it. Yet this is the gap in logic that underlies the case for the Welfare State. There may have been a case for localised experiments in state education or government medicine, etc; but the Fabian/Beveridge/Titmuss argument was, in effect if not in intention, to replace the imperfect market by the still more imperfect state, because it replaced imperfect but corrigible competition by virtually self-perpetuating state monopoly. The state may be able to make competition less imperfect in industry; but once the state has a monopoly it is very difficult to remove it.

Yet the argument, that because the market in welfare was imperfect it should be replaced by the state, had been built into the consolidation of the monolithic Welfare State in 1948. This was the case we set out to test. But we encountered an unexpected obstruction. No matter how convincing the counter-argument for alternatives to state monopoly in welfare, it seemed destined to be fruitless.

The Institute's early studies of government services—by Arthur Seldon in pensions (1957), by Norman Macrae in housing (1960), by Professor Dennis Lees in health (1961), by A. P. Herbert and Ralph Harris in libraries (1962), by Professor A. R. Ilersic in local government (1963), and other subjects[1]—were met by an almost uniformly sceptical response from people in all parties, including (with notable exceptions) Conservative-inclined people then in office in the 1955 to 1964 Conservative Governments. The knowing reaction was that, although the argument was persuasive, little or nothing could be done to replace undesirable policies because the desirable policies were 'politically impossible'. It was 'politically impossible' to replace state pensions, despite their dangers, by private pensions, despite their advantages. It was 'politically impossible' to do much about rent restriction despite its devastating

[1] A list of IEA studies in social policy is in Appendix F.

effects on housing. It was 'politically impossible' to do much about the National Health Service despite its intensifying weaknesses. It was 'politically impossible' to do anything about local government libraries despite their abuses and wastes. It was 'politically impossible' to do anything about the rising rates required to pay for growing local government in general. Reform, even if incontrovertible and desirable, was 'politically impossible'. *Impasse.*

Since the early 1960s this objection has continued from Conservative-inclined to Liberal-inclined and Labour-inclined people as the political colour of government changed in 1964, 1970 and 1974. Again there were notable exceptions, but the few independent spirits in all three parties did not speak out in public, and were swamped by their conventional-minded confrères.[2]

If we had been persuaded, awed or stampeded by this objection from public men who claimed to know which policies the sovereign people would welcome or accept, we might have withdrawn or developed a very different kind of Institute. It would have relied for advice not on independent economists disquieted by post-war trends and ready to contemplate radical solutions but on knowing politicians, practical administrators, retired civil servants; and it would have concentrated on subjects and approaches in which the conclusions for policy that emerged would have been regarded by these advisers as 'politically possible'. The results would have been sterile. This was how other institutes in Britain

---

[2] The discouraging response of politicians and other pragmatists to early and later IEA studies of state welfare is reviewed in Ralph Harris and Arthur Seldon, *Not from Benevolence . . .*, Hobart Paperback 10, IEA, 1977.

(and abroad) have worked. Some have declined or have been kept alive by the artificial respiration of 'public' funds—taxpayers' money on which taxpayers have not been consulted.

THE UNACCEPTABLE PRE-JUDGEMENT

For several reasons the 'politically impossible' objection was itself unacceptable. First, it seemed to us to be the natural response of politicians who did not relish opposition and of officials who relished a quiet life. The 'political' difficulty in espousing radical reform was clear enough: the beneficiaries from preserving existing policies undisturbed were clearly identifiable and concentrated—from recipients of state benefits in cash or kind to officials who administered the system. The benefits were obvious and real. The prospective beneficiaries from reform were in contrast widely dispersed: they were the whole nation of taxpayers, who could hardly miss what they had never known. Politicians were therefore least inclined to espouse reforms where the losses were concentrated and the gains dispersed, and, moreover, where motives could easily be mis-represented: anyone who questioned state welfare was likely to be reviled as lacking compassion.

Thomas Hobbes, the 17th-century philosopher, described anarchy as the war of all against all (*bellum omnes contra omnes*). This is a more accurate insight into the jockeying of interest groups in the Welfare State for the fruits of taxation than is the Utopian vision that it would bring universal brotherhood. The late Professor R. M. Titmuss, a critic of the IEA, dreamed of a 'badge of citizenship' worn by everyone in the Welfare State, since all would be concerned about the well-being of all

others. Universal selflessness is devoutly to be wished;
the error is to suppose it has arrived, or can be created
by the state. The reality is almost the opposite. The
increasing realisation that everyone is paying taxes for
welfare benefits induces everyone to take not as little as
he must, but as much as he can. It encourages everyone
to draw as much in benefits as he can, and contribute in
taxes as little as he cannot evade. Hobbes's law of the
jungle is a truer description of the Welfare State than
are the soothing formulae of its advocates.

Our proposals were 'politically impossible', therefore,
not because the *public* did not want them but because
the *politicians* would require effort and run risks to
demonstrate their advantages in practice. The difficulty
was not that the reforms were 'politically impossible'
but that the politicians and officials could not be
expected to adopt reforms that risked their personal
comfort even though the public would benefit.

We had thus in the early 1960s stumbled on the
realisation, later formulated and developed by Professor
Gordon Tullock,[3] that it was unrealistic to adopt the
still prevailing conventional wisdom of political science
and public administration (but also among eminent
economists like Keynes)[4] which held that politicians
were benevolent despots and bureaucrats were 'obedient
servants'[5] who lived only to serve the public interest.
The economist analysing public policy and emerging

[3] *The Politics of Bureaucracy,* Public Affairs Press, Washington,
DC, 1965.

[4] J. M. Buchanan, J. Burton, R. E. Wagner, *The Consequences
of Mr Keynes,* Hobart Paper 78, IEA, 1978.

[5] A student/colleague of Tullock was Professor William A.
Niskanen, who developed an economic theory of how bureau-
[*Continued on page 11*]

with conclusions for reform has to regard politicians and bureaucrats as no different from anyone else; they, too, try to maximise the return they most desire from their activities—whether in purchasing power, political power, prestige, spiritual satisfaction, or any other desired form. We did not, in 1963, pause to construct a theory of political or bureaucratic behaviour. It was sufficient that we were not persuaded by the paradoxical and puzzling objection that reform which IEA authors argued could be in the public interest—and which the objectors scarcely attempted to refute—was nevertheless 'politically impossible'.

Second, the objection seemed faulty because it was arguing in a circle, assuming what it had to prove. If a direction, or re-direction, of research and inquiry were excluded because the reforms it indicated were thought 'politically impossible', it would never be put to the test in practice. If, for example, research into alternative methods of financing health services privately outside the National Health Service were suppressed as 'unacceptable', these methods would never be created, refined and offered as an alternative *for the public to experience and reject if found wanting*. Even limited experimentation would therefore be excluded.

Third, moreover, the notion of 'political impossibility' pre-judges the public reception of a new idea, since, as Keynes taught, economic thinking is itself part

[*Continued from page 10*]
cracy burgeoned, succinctly summarised in *Bureaucracy: Servant or Master?*, Hobart Paperback 5, IEA, 1973. Another theory, evolved by Professor Albert Breton in *The Economic Theory of Representative Government*, Aldine, Chicago, 1974, was elaborated in *The Economics of Politics*, IEA Readings No. 18, IEA, 1978.

of the process by which policy is evolved. Politicians do not invariably put the public interest before their own, though they would like intellectual support for whatever policy they promote, and they deploy patronage to elicit a supply of testimonials. Academic supply has responded to the political 'demand' for validation of harmful policies of state welfare, which have damaged not least the people they most sought to help. And the blame must be shared by leader-writers who encouraged politicians of all parties to claim that their policies were in the public interest, without telling their readers of the alternatives, which were in effect concealed by the unjustified assumption that they were 'politically impossible'.

The 'politically impossible' objection, in short, was based on opinion without evidence. And, since the opinion was that of people who thought they stood to lose from change, it could not be accepted without evidence from the public itself.

The importance of *ignoring* the 'politically impossible' straitjacket, following through the analysis to its logical conclusions, and not pre-judging the question of political possibility or impossibility, was thereafter emphasised as an indispensable ingredient in commissioning the economists invited to write *Hobart* and other IEA *Papers*.

Later in the 1960s, when the objection proved stubborn, we asked Professor W. H. Hutt to examine it thoroughly. The result was the first of the *Hobart Paperbacks,* published in 1971, *Politically Impossible . . .?* This series was created to trace the processes through which ideas eventually influenced policy or, more relevant to this inquiry into welfare policy, were neglected without being rebutted.

NEW RESEARCHES

In 1962 we refused to be discouraged by the objection and, on the contrary, decided to test it by the only method available—the sampling techniques of opinion polling and market research, with several innovations to remove the defects of 'priceless' surveys that asked opinions without prices. Despite early teething troubles, condemnation by politicians (the late R. H. S. Crossman, Mrs Shirley Williams), and scepticism by social administrators (Professor Peter Townsend, Professor Gordon Forsyth[6]), the method has stood the test of time. In a word, we rejected the judgement of politicians and officials. We went over their heads to the public who, they claimed, would not welcome the radical reforms to which IEA authors were led by their analyses of the failures of government in supplying pensions, housing, health services, education and local government services in general without markets.

POLITICIANS OUT OF TOUCH WITH PUBLIC PREFERENCES

The results of our surveys in 1963, 1965, 1970 and now in 1978 indicated that the politicians and officials were wrong. The findings of these researches, moreover, show a 15-year trend in public preferences that reveals the objection of 'political impossibility' to be *increasingly* unfounded, until in 1978 it has become a myth. And if we project the trend into the 1980s, the reforms which have emerged from IEA studies in these 15 years can be seen to be not only increasingly 'politically possible' but, even more, politically overdue. Indeed

[6] *Doctors and State Medicine,* Pitman, 1966 (2nd edition, 1973).

the longer they are delayed the more the evolving demand by the public for a choice outside the state will be suppressed, and the more coercion the state will have to exert to prevent it breaking out in attempts by the people to escape from the state, whether by paying from taxed income for private services (which the lower-income families cannot do as readily as others), emigration or defiance by tax avoidance and evasion as a *quid pro quo* for the imposition of payment for an unacceptable state service.

RIGHT/LEFT 'BIAS'?

For some time it was thought that the IEA's interest in markets indicated a 'right-wing'[7] approach that concealed a political bias. Since there has been increasingly assiduous study of the market by economists in Communist countries for 20 years, the imputation of bias was itself tendentious. Even so, criticism of the IEA field surveys tended to come from the Left rather than from the Right, chiefly, perhaps, because there is usually more intellectual curiosity on the Left than on the Right and more alertness to the power of new ideas. Sociologists on the Left tend also to be offended by the notion that welfare might be supplied more effectively in the market than by government, which on the paternalist Left no less than on the patrician Right is incurably supposed to be controlled by benevolent despots and run by sea-green incorruptible officials, if not by themselves.

[7] Although convenient, 'Right' and 'Left' continue to be misleading, if not mischievous, as Samuel Brittan argued in *Left or Right: the Bogus Dilemma,* Secker & Warburg, 1968.

It should therefore be emphasised that the IEA field surveys could have been welcomed more on the Left than on the Right. Professor Brian Abel-Smith, a leading Titmuss lieutenant, and until lately an adviser to the Department of Health and Social Security, had long argued that the articulate middle classes derived more benefit from 'free' state welfare services than did the inarticulate working classes. Not only the thus favoured consumers of state welfare but also its controllers (politicians, civil servants, local councillors, officials) and employees (doctors, architects, teachers) were often Conservative-inclined and would not welcome disturbance in the National Health Service, state education, or council housing. Not least, real incomes during this period were rising proportionately more among the Labour-inclined, wage-paid, semi-skilled and skilled workers than among the Conservative-inclined, salaried, white-collar administrators and managers, and it was therefore among Labour Party supporters that the urge to pay for a better service than the state could claim to supply equally out of taxation would develop most strongly.

Among Labour politicians this emerging trend was seen most clearly by a former *Tribune* leader-writer, Mr Raymond Fletcher, Labour MP for the mining constituency of Ilkeston in Derbyshire. Two years after he entered Parliament in 1964 he wrote in *The Times*:

'The workers . . . have little enthusiasm for an expansion of the social wage at the expense of their individual wage packets . . .'

'In the last two decades [i.e. since the 1939-45 war] their collective aspirations have waned and their individual aspirations have waxed . . .'

'. . . hostility to the tax collector has increased.'

It is true that R. H. S. Crossman, advised by Professor Townsend, condemned the first report in 1963, and incautiously accused us of selecting the sample to produce the results he said we wanted.[8] And Mrs Shirley Williams, whose reactions and policies belie her cultivated reputation as a 'moderate', condemned the report on TV as 'nonsense'. Both may have sensed the findings as politically embarrassing. But a Labour MP wrote privately:

> 'Your researches have firmly established what I myself had derived from contact with my constituents . . . the glacial shift in working class attitudes since 1948 which my party colleagues, especially those who boast of their 'grass roots', cannot see . . .'

1963 TO 1978

This was the origin of these field researches, with which we persevered despite the early hostile reception based more on ideological dismay at the unexpected findings than on technical criticism of the methodology.

The second report came in 1965. It indicated a two-year trend against the state and in favour of the market. To see if the trend was established or if the 1963-65 movement was exceptional, we waited for five years before the third survey in 1970. The same trend was again revealed.

We thought then that we had done enough to identify

[8] The sample was decided in consultation with Mr Leonard England, then of Mass-Observation, who has advised on and conducted all the surveys. Mr Crossman withdrew his allegation.

an unsuspected[9] trend and could leave it to other economists to analyse and for government to reflect on public policy if, as it claimed, it existed to serve the public interest. In 1978, following the IEA Seminar on *The Economics of Politics*, at which Professor J. M. Buchanan had appraised the attempt by economists, led by Professor Kenneth Arrow, to create a 'social welfare function'[10] that assembled individual orders of preference for government to deploy in planning the use of resources, it seemed that the methods we had evolved to measure preferences between state and private services could be used to discover how far individual preferences on the expenditure of (their) taxes on government services were reflected in politicians' 'priorities'. The results are reviewed in Chapter 6.

The opportunity was also taken to repeat the main micro-choice and macro-choice questions and so to discover if the 7-year trend from 1963 to 1970 had continued for 8 more years to 1978. (It had.)

---

[9] 'Unsuspected' because other social surveys claimed to have found widespread approval of state welfare services: Chapter 5, pp. 79-80. It is not implied that government must reflect public opinion on every issue. Hanging is the familiar example of a policy on which it is argued public feeling—'gusts of passion'—should not necessarily determine policy. The personal concerns of husbands and wives for each other and for their children go to the roots of family life and cannot be regarded as transient moods that government can lightly ignore.

[10] The relevance of the 'social welfare function' is indicated in a Note to Chapter 6.

CHAPTER 2

Proposition 13, GB:
Would You Like a Limit on Taxes?

Are the people of Britain satisfied with the machinery of elections as the means of showing their *individual* preferences in welfare and how to pay for it?

In June 1978 the people of California were enabled, by a unique constitutional technique, the 'initiative', to vote directly for a change in the constitution by simple majority. The 'initiative' requires an amendment or proposition to be placed on the election ballot by a petition with the required number of signatories.

Proposition 13 was such an amendment; it was passed by 65% of the votes recorded to limit the property taxes (which we call 'rates') on real estate. It provided that the maximum tax should be one per cent of its value, that the rise in value could be assessed at no more than 2 per cent a year, and that these rules of taxation could be changed only by a two-thirds majority in both houses of the California legislature.

In Britain Parliament is sovereign. There is no written constitution to limit its powers to raise taxation to any rate or amount it can vote through the House of Commons by a simple majority of MPs, who may represent a minority of voters. It does not ask the electorate if it thinks taxation should be limited to any maximum or by any formula. Parliament can push taxation as high as it thinks fit subject only, perhaps, to adverse public reaction in the loss of its votes at the next General Election, the loss of revenue by tax avoidance and evasion, emigration or ultimately revolution.[1]

Hitherto in Britain, ballot-box voting has been the only public sign of disapproval a Parliament had to fear; but it was a blunt instrument, since the British public could not, unlike the people of California, vote on taxation alone, but had to add it to many other policies—possibly from home rule for Northern Ireland to vivisection. Tax avoidance and evasion has been an instrument of protest and escape the British have used increasingly for 10 years or more. Emigration has also been used, although it is a drastic response with a high cost in separation from family, friends and country. Revolution has been fomented or exacerbated by taxation in England in 1381 (the Wat Tyler rebellion), in 1688 (the Glorious Revolution), the USA in 1776, France in 1789, Germany, Italy, etc. in 1848. Although it may seem improbable and remote, rebellion against high taxation cannot be ruled out in present-day England.[2] It has begun and spread in the form of tax evasion in the resistance variously described as the

[1] Professor C. K. Rowley, in *The State of Taxation,* Readings 16, IEA, 1977, discusses the forms of political 'participation' citizens who feel coerced might adopt: voting, pressure-group formation, social movements leading to new political parties or civil disobedience, individual adjustment such as tax evasion, revolution or migration.

[2] The resistance has been more explicit in local government. A protest meeting in Islington, organised by the Chartered Union of Taxpayers (CUT), resolved to withhold rates. A demonstration of 1,500 ratepayers at Islington Town Hall in March 1979 persuaded the Council to cut its proposed increase in rates from 40% to 32%.

hidden, grey or underground economy. And trade union power was used to rebel against the high taxation of (constricted) wages in 1979 that wage-earners evidently do not regard as compensated by the social wage.

The extent of tax evasion is evidently much larger than is commonly recognised. Sir William Pile, Chairman of the Board of the Inland Revenue, has applied the term 'black economy' to the activities of moonlighters with second jobs, paid in cash, and not recorded in income tax returns. His estimate is that such income may amount to £10 billion or $7\frac{1}{2}\%$ of the GNP.[3] (If, as seems likely, such tax evasion has been spreading in recent years, the growth in the British GNP has been less sluggish than is generally supposed.)

Short of government concessions or other reforms to remove the causes of such rebellious reactions, it is still possible for private organisations to exercise initiative in discovering the strength of public resentment against rising taxation. Questions on limitation of taxation (and therefore government expenditure) more or less on the lines of Proposition 13 in California were therefore added to the 1978 survey.

A LIMIT TO GOVERNMENT EXPENDITURE
AND TAXATION

Two questions were originally devised. The first was:

'In Britain as in California recently should we be allowed to vote for a limit on government expenditure? Do you agree strongly, agree, neither agree nor disagree, disagree, or disagree strongly?'

[3] *Financial Weekly,* 30 March 1979.

The wording referred to a limit on government *expenditure* rather than, as in California, to a limit on *taxation*. The results were: agree strongly 11 per cent, agree 45 per cent, neither 13 per cent, disagree 26 per cent, disagree strongly 4 per cent: in summary 56 per cent

Table I
Desire for Referenda on Limiting Government Expenditure and Taxation: GB, 1978

Base	Survey I 1,992 aged 16 to 65 (July/August 1978) (Question 21)*		Survey II 1,856 aged 18+ (November 1978) (Question 1)†	
	Vote on referendum on limiting government expenditure		Referendum on limiting taxation	
	% of sample	% of 'votes' cast	% of sample	% of 'votes' cast
In favour	56	65	59	73
Against/not in favour	30	34	22	27
Neither/Don't know	13	—	19	—

*The main (July/August) questionnaire is reproduced at Appendix A.

†The three-question November questionnaire is reproduced at Appendix B.

agreed, 30 per cent did not. This was an almost two-to-one majority in favour of a 'referendum' on a limit on, and therefore on the extent of, government expenditure (Table I and Chart A).

The second question was:

'In California recently two people out of three voted to reduce taxation and accept fewer services. If there was a vote in this country on the same issue, would you vote for or against?'

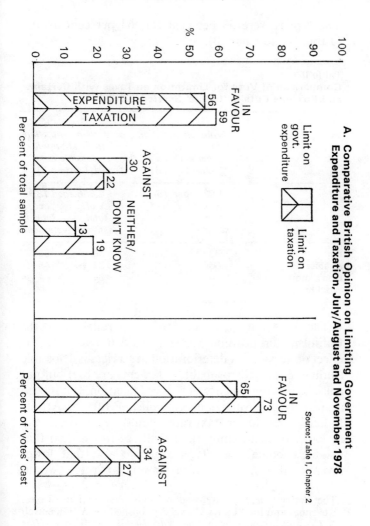

A. Comparative British Opinion on Limiting Government Expenditure and Taxation, July/August and November 1978

Source: Table I, Chapter 2

The replies were 33 per cent for, 63 per cent against
(Table II and Chart B).

Table II
**Comparison of Vote for Limitation on Taxes with Certain
and Possible Cuts in 'Public' Services: GB, 1978**

	Survey I 'Vote' on limitation on taxation with certain cuts (Question 26)		Survey II 'Vote' on limitation on taxation with possible cuts (Question 3)	
Base	1,992 aged 16-65		1,856 aged 18+	
	% of total sample	% of total 'votes' cast	% of total sample	% of total 'votes' cast
For	33	34	33	55
Against	63	66	27	45
Don't know	4	—	34	—
Would not vote	—	—	6	—

The question was not strictly parallel with the
California Proposition 13, which did not refer to the
effect on services. A deterioration in services is a possible
(though eventually probable if tax cuts are big) but not
a necessary consequence of reduced taxation. It has been
argued by the American economist, Professor Arthur
Laffer,[4] that lower tax rates could yield more tax
revenue, by sharpening the incentives to earn, so that
taxable income rises. It is arguable also that lower
revenue, if it resulted from lower tax rates, would

[4] The Laffer Curve is discussed by Jude Wanniski in 'Taxes,
Revenues and the "Laffer Curve",' published by W. Greenwell
& Co and adapted from *The Way The World Works: How
Economies Fail and Succeed*, Basic Books, New York, 1978.

B. GB Opinion on Limitation on Government Spending and Taxation according to certainty and possibility of cuts in Services, 1978

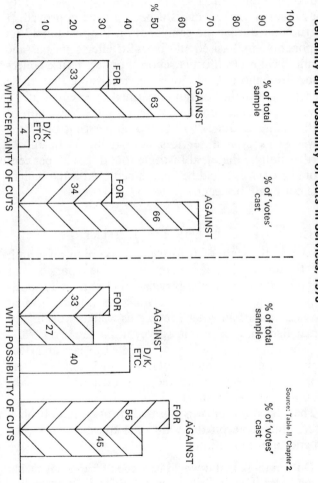

Source: Table II, Chapter 2

induce economy in government and leave the quality
(or range) of services undisturbed, or even improved. It
is true that during the campaign on Proposition 13 its
opponents emphasised the harmful effects its passage
would have on California schools, police, refuse collection, fire-fighting and other services, and that these
warnings—whether or not confirmed by events—might
have had an effect on the voting. (A CBS News poll of
Californians in June 1978 found 60 per cent preferred
lower taxes even if services were reduced. In July a
further poll by the Field Institute found that 38 per cent
thought services could be maintained even if the budget
was cut by 40 per cent.)

OPINION OF VOTERS ON TAX LIMITATION

To assess the state of British public opinion on a limit
on taxation without reference to the (possible or
certain) effect on public services (the issue in Proposition 13), questions were formulated for a national
cross-section of all voters, retired as well as working, in
Great Britain, in a second survey in November 1978.

The sample was 1,856 people aged 18 years and over
representing GB voters totalling 40·5 million. The
sample and the numbers they represent in each sub-
group are shown in the Table opposite.

The first question was phrased to ask opinion on a
referendum vote on the California question: *tax* (not
expenditure) limitation:

> 'Do you think that it would be a good idea or not such a
> good idea if we in Britain, as in California recently, had
> a referendum or special vote on reducing taxation to a
> maximum proportion or limit?'

'Proposition 13, GB' Survey			Equivalent population (million)
Total	1,856	electors	40·5
Men	863		18·8
Women	993		21·7
Age: 18-24	199		4·3
25-34	389		8·5
35-54	562		12·3
55+	706		15·4
Occupational: AB	303		6·6
C1	408		8·9
C2	604		13·2
DE	541		11·8
Voting intention: Con.	686		15·0
Lab.	758		16·5
Lib.	72		1·6
Don't know, other	340		7·4

Note: The sample was 'stratified' and random: electors' names were drawn from the electoral register (and non-electors aged 15 to 18 years were chosen by a systematic method). The sample was drawn from 178 constituencies, with 18 or 20 names from each (with a 65% response rate). The survey was conducted by NOP Market Research Ltd.

59 per cent of the sample thought it was 'a good idea', 22 per cent 'not such a good idea', 19 per cent said 'don't know'. The figures are shown in Table I with the vote in favour of limiting government expenditure. And both sets of figures are recalculated as percentages of the votes cast.

Men and women returned similar percentages of the sample for approval. Younger people were rather more in favour than older people.[5] Perhaps strangely, the AB and C1 occupational groups were less in favour than

---

[5] As with the main Survey I, the full computer tabulations for Survey II are available from the IEA for a charge.

the C2 and DE groups.[6] The rising working classes (C2) were more in favour than any other social group (66 per cent). But there was no difference at all between people intending to vote Conservative and Labour. This is possibly the most surprising finding of all. If, as is universally thought, the public services are the bastion of the lower-paid, they would be expected to be much less for a Proposition 13 vote to limit taxes than the other groups who are supposed to pay for public services by their high taxes. Yet people in the sample with Labour intentions were just as much in favour of a GB Proposition 13 as were people with Conservative intentions.

In all, 22 per cent disapproved of a vote on limiting taxes for reasons that were not asked but which would have been revealing to learn. Some clues may be derived from the analysis by sub-group. Men were much more opposed than women, not because more women were in favour but because more replied 'don't know'. The youngest (18-24) were more in favour than the less young (25-34), and the middle-aged (35-54) less in favour than the older (55 and over).

The most marked difference in opposition was in the occupational groups: AB 43 per cent, C1 28 per cent, C2 18 per cent, DE 11 per cent. This result is puzzling. In contrast with the expectation that the most highly taxed would most favour the opportunity of voting to limit taxation, and the least taxed would oppose it most, the results were precisely the opposite.

Question 2 attempted to reproduce the content of

---

[6] These groups are explained in Appendix C. They are based on occupations rather than incomes, although the two are broadly related.

Proposition 13 by omitting qualifications about the effect, if any, on public services:

'If there were such a referendum would you vote for or against such a maximum proportion or limit?'

Fifty-seven per cent said they would vote in favour, 15 per cent against. The 57 per cent of the British sample *of all voters* compared with the 65 per cent of the electorate *who voted* in California. (California and GB are compared in Table III and Chart C.) The arguments for

Table III
Comparison of Votes on Tax Limitation, 'Proposition 13', USA and GB

Base	USA: California	GB	
	All votes cast*	Survey II Sample 1,856 of whom 72% 'voted'	
		% of sample	% of 'votes' cast
For	65	57	79
Against	35	15	21
Don't know/Would not vote	—	27	—

*In total 4·19 million in favour, 2·28 million against.

and against were put fully and forcefully in several weeks of spirited campaigning by both sides in the USA, and the voters could be said to be more fully informed than the GB sample, which had not answered the earlier questions in the main survey. Nevertheless the two votes are broadly comparable. The vote against in Britain was 15 per cent, much less than in California, where it was 35 per cent. Moreover the British proportions in favour

**C. GB-USA (California) Comparison of Opinion on Tax
Limitation, 1978**

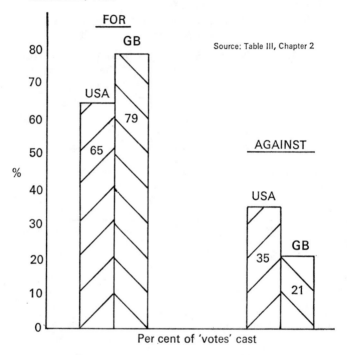

Source: Table III, Chapter 2

Per cent of 'votes' cast

were even larger: in California the vote in favour was
two to one (65 per cent: 35 per cent), in Britain nearly
four to one (57 per cent: 15 per cent). When recalculated
as percentages of the votes cast to make them comparable with the California referendum figures of votes cast,
the vote in favour rose to nearly 80 per cent.

Again there were several interesting features in the
differences between the sub-groups. The men were
rather more in favour of limiting taxation than the

women. The three younger age groups were very similar, and the oldest much less in favour. Once more, the C2 group stood out as most in favour of limiting taxes. This again is a remarkable feature, although it was perhaps to be expected in view of their stronger preference than all other groups for having a tax referendum like Proposition 13 at all.

The political analysis was also intriguing, and perhaps disturbing to the hypothesis that public services do the lower paid good. People with Labour intentions voted 59 per cent in favour of limiting taxes, much the same as the 61 per cent with Conservative intentions. Perhaps the psephologists can explain these figures in political terms. For economists who have studied the social services, social trends and social aspirations, the high Labour result—'the Fletcher effect' (page 15)—is not surprising.

OPINION IF TAX LIMITATION CUT SERVICES

Since tax limitation, if it proceeds far enough, might or would cut services, the third question repeated the second and added the qualification on public services:

'If there were such a referendum would you vote for or against such a maximum proportion or limit even if, as a result, government might cut some services?'

Here 33 per cent, many fewer than the 57 per cent for unqualified tax limitation, said they would still vote in favour of tax limitation even if there was a prospect (not certainty) of a cut in public services: they are shown in Table IV. This percentage is the same as the response to the original question (Table II, page 24) which said cuts were certain, and might therefore have been expected to be higher. That it was not may be explained by the in-

Table IV
Comparison of Votes on Tax Limitation with and without possible Cuts in Services
Base: Total sample representing all voters 18+

| | Survey II Possible cuts in services | | | |
| | without (Question 2) | | with (Question 3) | |
	% of sample	% of 'votes' cast	% of sample	% of 'votes' cast
For	57	79	33	55
Against	15	21	27	45
Don't know/ Would not vote	27	—	40	—

clusion in Survey II of the oldest voters who draw pensions and have transport and other concessions and may be more apprehensive of tax limitation than middle-aged or younger people.

But the vote against was even less—27 per cent. This is also very much less than the 63 per cent against in the original question in Survey I (Table II). There was thus a small majority in favour of tax limitation even if public services might be cut. And if these figures are recalculated in terms of the votes cast there is a sizeable majority in favour (55 per cent to 45 per cent, Table IV).

These figures suggest, contrary to political notions (Ch. 5), that the British are capable of making consistent judgements on tax reduction according to whether the 'price' in public services is high or low. They behave like rational beings according to the law of demand that the lower the price the more they will want, or pay for.

They are better at making such judgements than some politicians seem to think. They do not give mutually conflicting replies if they are told the price. They can intelligently decide between paying their taxes for government to spend or keeping their money and spending it themselves.

The large difference in the non-voters in Table II is explained by a difference in the wording of the questions. The question in Survey I invited only replies 'for' and 'against'. The questions in Survey II more realistically gave the further options: 'Don't know' and 'Would not vote'. It is possible that people not in favour of a British revolutionary innovation of putting a limit on government expenditure or taxation voted 'against' in Survey I and 'don't know' in Survey II: that would explain the much higher 63 per cent in Survey I than the 27 per cent in Survey II. If so, the 'don't knows' could not be divided more or less equally between 'for' and 'against', as is often found to be valid in other social surveys. This supposition is confirmed by a further analysis of the replies,[7] which indicates that most respondents who were in favour of a limit on taxes as such (without cuts in services) changed their minds to 'don't know' when the possibility of cuts in services was introduced. Their ultimate decision would, sensibly, depend on the extent of the expected cuts (i.e. the 'price' of the tax cuts). If the cuts seemed likely to be extensive, presumably more would oppose tax limitation; if the cuts seemed likely to be minor, presumably more would support tax limitation.

A further difference is that the sample for Survey I stopped at the formal retirement age for men (65), while

[7] Available with the main computer sheets.

Survey II included all voters up to all ages. The sub-group analysis shows that the older people (55+) were rather more inclined to oppose a limit on taxation with or without the possibility of fewer services.

In the meantime, to see how the results would appear in a referendum, and to compare the attitudes to limitation on government expenditure and on tax with possible cuts in services, the replies are shown in Table II recalculated as percentages of the votes cast (excluding 'don't knows'). Thus, the referendum on limiting government expenditure with the *certainty* of service cuts drew a 96 per cent vote, of which 34 per cent were for and 66 per cent against. The referendum on limiting taxation with *possible* service cuts, which we have argued (p. 33) is the more realistic proposition, drew a 60 per cent vote, of which 55 per cent were in favour and 45 per cent against (Table IV). This was a clear margin in favour of putting a limit to taxation. Reproduced on a national scale, as it would be if the samples are accurate cross-sections of the (voting) population, it would show a clear majority in favour of tax limitation despite the absence of prompting from any of the political parties. Tax limitation would sooner or later severely discipline government, once its tempta-tion to over-borrow had been tempered by a new fiscal constitution to control unbalanced budgeting, as trench-antly argued by Professor J. M. Buchanan,[8] by more systematic pricing of personal services unnecessarily supplied by government, as we have argued elsewhere,[9] and perhaps by abolishing the government monopoly of

---

[8] *The Consequences of Mr Keynes,* Hobart Paper 78, IEA, 1978.
[9] *Pricing or Taxing?,* Hobart Paper 71, 1976.

money supply, and so stopping monetary incontinence once for all, as proposed by Professor F. A. Hayek.[10]

WHO WANTS LIMITS ON GOVERNMENT AND TAXES?

The most interesting difference in the working sub-groups was that 61 per cent of the C2DE group favoured a referendum on limiting government expenditure against 50 per cent of the ABC1 group; and 58 per cent of the less (or shorter) educated were in favour against 50 per cent of those with longer education. On the other hand, 60 per cent of Conservative sympathisers favoured a referendum against 53 per cent of Labour sympathisers. Again occupational 'class' overlapped with political sympathy, some of the wage-paid and the shorter-educated evidently voting as Conservative sympathisers, and the salaried and longer-educated voting as Labour sympathisers.

The largest difference in the working sample in the vote for or against a limit on government taxation *with fewer 'public' services* was between the party sympathies: 44 per cent Conservatives would vote in favour contrasted with 23 per cent Labour. Conversely, 76 per cent of Labour sympathisers would vote against, compared with 52 per cent Conservative. Since the ABC1s voted only marginally more in favour than the C2DEs, the Conservatives again must have contained people with lower incomes and shorter education, and Labour sympathisers people with higher incomes and longer education.

The four occupational group sub-divisions for the

[10]*Denationalisation of Money*, Hobart Paper 70, 1976 (2nd Edition, 1978).

vote amongst all voters on a referendum to limit taxation (without reference to the effect on public services)
reveals that the C2s were especially strongly in favour—
more than any other sub-group (66 per cent)—and the
ABs least in favour (47 per cent). Indeed the C2s were
more than three to one in favour of a vote (66 per cent
against 18 per cent) while the ABs, the highest-taxed,
were only slightly in favour (47 per cent against 43 per
cent). Yet the party groups showed almost no difference
at all: Conservatives, Labour and Liberals were all at
61 to 62 per cent in favour and around 18 to 23 per cent
against. The desire for a vote to limit taxation thus ran
equally through all political sympathies but was
markedly stronger among the relatively lower-income
groups and lower-taxed. Since living standards have
generally risen more among the C2s than among the
ABs, the result suggests that the attitude to taxation may
be related not to absolute income (and therefore tax paid)
but to the rate of increase in income (and therefore in
tax) in recent years. The people who are most opposed
to high taxes are evidently not those with highest
incomes (many of whom may be of Labour sympathy)
but those whose incomes have risen fastest (and who
may be moving to Conservative sympathy).

TAX CUTS WITH AND WITHOUT CUTS IN PUBLIC SERVICES

This difference is supported by the replies on limiting
tax (without reference to the effect, if any, on public
services). Again the C2s were more in favour (62 per
cent) than any other social group and the ABs least
(52 per cent). And again the Conservative and Labour

sympathisers had almost the same figures, near 60 per cent.

Other differences appeared in the vote when the possibility of cuts in services was introduced. Men remained much more in favour than women. But the percentages in favour were about the same in all occupational groups, while many fewer C2s (28 per cent) than ABs (38 per cent) were opposed. Labour supporters also fell away (to 32 per cent) more than Conservatives (to 39 per cent).

The large proportion of 'don't knows' may have been mostly opposed to tax cuts, but the extent of their opposition would vary with the extent of the anticipated cuts in services. If the figures are read as a

Table V
GB Referendum on Limits to Taxation

	USA: California Limit on taxes (no reference to cuts in services)	GB Limit on taxes (with possible cuts in services) (Survey II, Question 3)						
			Social Group				Political Sympathy		
		AB	C1	C2	DE	Con.	Lab.	Lib.
Base:	All Groups	Total Sample: 1,856						
	%	%	%	%	%	%	%	%
For	65	48	55	55	61	63	51	62
Against	35	51	45	45	39	37	49	40

referendum, where only the votes cast count in deciding opinion, the proportion in the sub-groups as percentages of the votes cast would be as shown in Table V (supposing that the neutrals and 'don't knows' do not vote).

There was therefore a majority of votes cast in favour of tax limitation in every socio-economic group except the ABs and in all three party sympathies. Such a result, if it were reproduced in a full national referendum, could hardly be ignored by government. But it is not able to emerge in the political machinery of representative government used in Britain at General Elections. One more unexpected result of this study is that it indicates a strong case for a referendum on whether or not referenda should be held not only on constitutional issues[11] like joining the EEC or devolution in Scotland and Wales but also on single issues of intimate personal consequence—taxes as well as social benefits. The outcome is hardly in doubt.

*   *   *

There seems little doubt, from these results, what the voting on a Proposition 13 in Britain would be. Perhaps that is why a referendum on taxes has never been proposed by politicians who require high tax revenue to finance high government expenditure, for reasons ranging from compassion (Mr Callaghan?) to a belief in the superior efficiency of government (Mr Wedgwood Benn?). And all the more surprising that politicians who would like to see lower taxation (Mr Jo Grimond? Sir Keith Joseph?) have not proposed it either.

But whatever the politicians believe or do, or fail to do, it would seem that the British are ready to

---

[11]The pros and cons of referenda and other direct franchises, and their use and results in Switzerland, the USA, Australia, France, Scandinavia, Ireland and the UK, are discussed in David Butler and Austin Ranney (eds.), *Referendums: A Comparative Study of Practice and Theory,* American Enterprise Institute, Washington, DC, 1978.

declare themselves in favour of limiting taxation, *even if it were to result in limiting the services supplied by government.*

How far would they limit government, not least in the two largest services it supplies in kind, education and medicine? Would they pay higher taxes for better state education or medicine? Or would they prefer lower taxes and pay privately? And do they approve of the allocation by government of tax revenue between the main components of state education and the National Health Service or would they want it allocated differently?

In 1978 we asked questions on both these sets of public preferences—the size of tax revenue for government to spend (Chapters 3 and 5), and the distribution by government of given tax revenues to see how far it reflected public preferences (Chapter 6). We now turn to review and analyse their replies to these questions, which are still not being asked by government itself.

CHAPTER 3

Your Verdict on Contracting Out

Politicians never ask the British public whether they are satisfied or dissatisfied with state welfare services in a manner that enables the voter to respond with an unequivocal 'yes' or 'no' to each main service. If asked, would voters indicate the general satisfaction that the perpetuation of present policies takes for granted? Would they echo Mrs Barbara Castle that the National Health Service is the envy of the world? Would they express satisfaction with state education? Or would they prefer to have their taxes refunded and go elsewhere for better value? (The state, unlike profit-making business, never says 'Satisfaction or your money back'.)

POLITICAL MARKET RESEARCH

To discover choice in education and medical care, the two largest 'benefits' in kind provided by government, we devised two kinds of test of preferences,[1] based on the two main methods of economic analysis and research: 'micro', the behaviour of individuals, and 'macro', the behaviour of large groups—a community or a country as a whole.

---

[1] Housing was the subject of a separate survey in 1968, supervised by the late Professor F. G. Pennance. Pensions were also investigated in the first three surveys but not included in the fourth because the two tests were not easy to apply to them.

The micro-test asked the sample how each individual would choose between state and private education and medical care. It asked: Which do *you* prefer? How would *you* act? The macro-test asked how he (or she) would choose between state policies for the people as a whole. It asked: Which policy do you prefer for *other* people as well as yourself?—for people generally? The micro-tests and their findings over the 15 years are discussed in Chapter 5, the macro-tests and their findings are reviewed in this Chapter.

In the general run of consumer goods and services, a producer remains in profitable business only by offering something that satisfies a sufficient part of the market better than competing suppliers. In contrast to the text-book models of 'static equilibrium', competition is constantly changing as new products, styles, shapes and selling methods are developed. There are few services like Post Office mail delivery which go on unchanging, or with deterioration, from decade to decade—and there would be still fewer if postal services were thrown open to the invigoration of competition.[2]

It is more credit to the market method than to the market men that producers are constantly compelled by competition to check whether some change in their product would improve its appeal to current or potential customers. A large part of the entrepreneurial function is in judging how far to risk the uncertainty that always attends the introduction of a new or 'improved' product; indeed the verdict on whether a change is an improvement depends on the preferences of the ultimately sovereign consumer. When a large investment is

[2] Ian Senior, *The Postal Service: Competition or Monopoly?*, Background Memorandum 3, IEA, 1970.

at stake, most business men have learned the wisdom of checking the judgements of their technical experts or the hunches of their salesmen by various forms of market research. By devising questionnaires under specialist guidance and inviting views on alternative products from a sufficient sample of potential customers, experience has shown that the answers can provide an indispensable (even if imperfect) guide to likely consumer behaviour in the market-place.

As students of the theory and practice of advertising and marketing[3] we therefore thought, when obstructed by the supposed consensus on state welfare and the alleged political impossibility of reform, that an obvious step was to examine whether the proven techniques of market research could be adapted to throw light on public preferences between state and competing welfare services in education and medical care. From the wide range of possible policies we decided, in consultation with our expert advisers, to formulate three distinctive options that reflected the debate between 'universal' and 'selective state welfare' and that could be applied to both education and medical care. Thus if there was to be a departure from the post-war approach of state-provided, tax-financed services available (so it is claimed[4]) equally for all, the alternatives for macro (national)-policy were broadly between the

[3] Ralph Harris and Arthur Seldon, *Advertising in a Free Society* (1959), *Advertising in Action* (1962), *Advertising and the Public* (1962), IEA.

[4] A large part of the case against 'universal' welfare has always been that medical facilities and, even more, schools differ widely in quality, and that the well-connected or more persistent with social push or political pull usually manage to get the best medical attention and education.

strict confinement of state support to people in need by requiring all others to pay directly for school fees, health insurance, etc, or the more gradual but still radical shift of policy by encouraging individual self-support in welfare through tax refunds or other devices. Both these alternatives to universal state welfare might be described as contracting out: either automatically by income (i.e. confined to families above a stipulated minimum) or by individual choice.

THE THREE OPTIONS

Accordingly, of the three formal options offered in our questionnaire, the first was for the continuation of the welfare state for all, whereby improvements would have to be financed from higher taxation. The second was the sharply contrasting approach of confining benefits to the poor and leaving the growing majority to look after themselves with the help of refunded or lower taxes. The third might be considered to offer a half-way house, although it is in principle the more libertarian alternative, of continuing state services but allowing *all* individuals the decision and choice of contracting out and spending their own money on welfare in the market. The precise questions asked in each of the four surveys, separately for health services and education, were as follows:

A 'The state should take more in taxes, rates and contributions and so on to pay for better or increased (health/education) services which everyone would have.'

B 'The state should take less in taxes, rates and contributions and so on to provide services only for people in need and leave others to pay or insure privately.'

C 'The state should continue the present service but allow people to contract out, pay less contributions and so on and use the money to pay for their own services.'

A. PREFERENCES IN HEALTH SERVICES

CHANGE FROM 1963 TO 1978

Since the question was put in identical terms in all four surveys, we can compare the preferences expressed over the 15 years as summarised in Table I. Even allowing that variations in the figures of a few percentage points may not be significant as falling within the statistical margin of error,[5] the picture presented in this first Table

Table I
Policy For Health: 1963-1978

Base: total sample	2,005	2,018	2,005	1,992	
	1963	1965	1970	1978	1978†
Policy Option*	%	%	%	%	%
A. Keep present system	41	32	29	20	22
B. Concentrate on poor	24	25	24	18	20
C. Allow contracting out	33	34	46	54	58
'Don't know'	2	9	1	7	—

*The full wording of the questions is stated above, pp. 44-5.
†Excluding 'don't knows'.

is of a remarkable, sustained shift away from support for the present universal system (declining from 41% to 20%) to support for permitting individual contracting out (rising from 33% to 54%). The more paternalistic change of concentrating state welfare on families

[5] Appendix D.

D. Choice in Health: 1963-1978

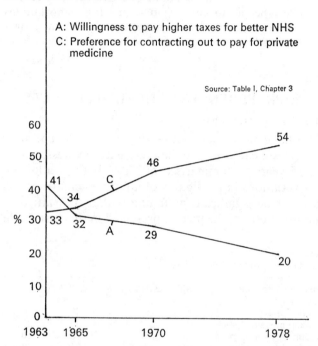

A: Willingness to pay higher taxes for better NHS
C: Preference for contracting out to pay for private medicine

Source: Table I, Chapter 3

in need was consistently least favoured in all four years and fell more moderately from 24-25% in the first three to 18% in 1978. (Chart D.)

TRENDS: 1963 TO 1970 TO 1978 . . .

Comparing the trend of change in preferences for the three options over the 15 years requires two factors to be borne in mind. The first is the lengthening interval between the surveys from two years between 1963 and 1965, five years between 1965 and 1970, and eight years between 1970 and 1978. If we take 1970 as roughly mid-way between 1963 and 1978, it appears that the rate of change away from support for option A (the present system) has been accelerating: it dropped by more than a quarter during the first half of the period (from 41% to 29%) and by approaching a third during the second half (from 29% to 20%). On the other hand, support for Option C (individual contracting out) increased more rapidly during the first half (from 33% in 1963 to 46% in 1970) than during the second half (from 46% to 54% in 1978).

. . . TO 1986?

This marked variation in the apparent rate of change draws attention to the second possibly distorting factor: the significant increase in 'don't knows' in 1978 (as also in 1965 which is omitted from the present discussion of trends between 1963-70 and 1970-78). If we confine the comparison to people expressing a positive choice between the three options—by ignoring 'don't knows' as non-voters are ignored in election results—support for the third option would rise in 1978 to 58% (in place of 54%). It is clear that this rate of increasing support for the radical-liberal option of permitting individual contracting out between 1963 and 1978 (from 33% to 58%, or by three-quarters) could not be maintained against the residual collectivist-conservative support for option A (the present system), since if this trend were projected for a further 15 years it would indicate around 100% support for option C by 1993. But even if we project the simple arithmetic increase of 25 percentage points from 1963 to 1978 for a further 15 years, the 58% favouring freedom to contract out would be above

80% by 1993. On a shorter time-horizon, the projection for 8 years of the increase between 1970 (46%) and 1978 (58%) would imply a vote for optional contracting out of around 70% by 1986.

COMPARISONS BY OCCUPATIONAL AND POLITICAL CATEGORIES

The indication of preferences by sub-group provides impressive support for the view that the implications of the choices were well understood by the men and

Table II
Policy for Health: Sex and Age Differences, 1978

Question 19	(Base: total sample 1,992)				
			Sex		Age
	All	Men	Women	16-34	35+
Policy Option	%	%	%	%	%
A. Keep present system	20	22	19	22	19
B. Concentrate on poor	18	19	17	19	17
C. Allow contracting out	54	53	57	52	56
'Don't know'	7	7	8	6	7

women questioned. Where Table II shows little variation by sex or age differences, Table III confirms that social occupational class (marginally) and party allegiance (significantly) influence the answers in the direction we would expect. In particular, Conservative sympathisers and the higher occupational groups (ABC1s)[6] are more markedly in favour of allowing individuals the option to contract out (58% in both cases) than Labour sympathisers (45%) and the lower occupational groups

[6] The occupational (or socio-economic, or 'class') groups are described in Appendix C.

Table III
Policy for Health: Occupational and Party Differences, 1978

Question 19	(Base: total sample 1,992)				
		Occupational Group		Party Sympathy	
	All	ABC1	C2DE	Con.	Lab.
Policy Option	%	%	%	%	%
A. Keep present system	20	20	21	18	28
B. Concentrate on poor	18	16	20	18	20
C. Allow contracting out	54	58	52	58	45
'Don't know'	7	6	7	6	7

(52%), and even less in favour of continuing the universal system—preferred by 18% of Conservative and 28% of Labour supporters. Compared, however, with the largest of these differences, the most impressive finding of the analysis by occupational group and political sympathy is that even of Labour supporters—who are most likely to feel committed to the post-war extension of universal welfare—70% (not counting 'don't knows') would in 1978 prefer contracting out, either automatically for those not in need (favoured by 22%) or by individual discretion (48%). If the same calculation is applied to the full sample, we find that the vote for one or other form of contracting out rose from 57% in 1963 to 78% in 1978 (Table I and Chart F).

B. PREFERENCES IN EDUCATION
CHANGES FROM 1963 TO 1978
The preferences analysed in Table IV show an even more marked collapse of support for present policies in education (from 51% in 1963 to 15% in 1978) than in health services. This falling away from the post-war

Table IV
Policy for Education: 1963-1978

Base: total sample	2,005	2,018	2,005	1,992	
	1963	1965	1970	1978	1978†
Policy Option	%	%	%	%	%
A. Keep present system	51	41	44	15	16
B. Concentrate on poor	20	16	20	17	19
C. Allow contracting-out	27	32	35	60	65
'Don't know'	2	11	2	8	—

†Excluding 'don't knows'.

consensus is almost exactly mirrored by the rapid increase in support for individual freedom to contract out which rose from 27% in 1963 to 60% in 1978.

TRENDS: 1963 TO 1970 TO 1978 . . .

A comparison with Table I reveals a still more emphatic change in the extent of support for governmental health and education services. Thus in 1963 state provision of education was more acceptable (51%) than of the National Health Service (41%). The same difference was even more visible in 1970 when 44% favoured option A (the present system) in education compared with 29% in health services. The most dramatic change in any of the figures over the full period of 15 years is seen since 1970 in education, where support for present policy (option A) plummeted by two-thirds from 44% to no more than 15%. Since, as in health, support for option B (concentration on the poor) remained more stable (between 16% and 20% throughout), the obverse of the decline in support for present policies in education since 1970 is seen in the increase by three-quarters of support for the individual option to contract out from 35% to 60%. It is difficult

E. Choice in Education, 1963-1978

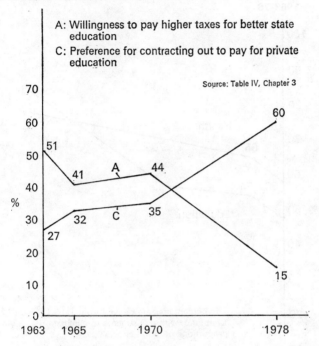

A: Willingness to pay higher taxes for better state education

C: Preference for contracting out to pay for private education

Source: Table IV, Chapter 3

to doubt that this accelerating change reflects wide-spread anxieties about standards of education in state schools and the increasing frustration of parental choice by the enforcement of comprehensive re-organisation in the face of spreading doubts about its universal effectiveness (Chart E).

. . . TO 1988?

It would scarcely be credible to project this recent rate of change in preferences into the future, not least because

F. **Support for Contracting Out in Health and Education, 1963-78**

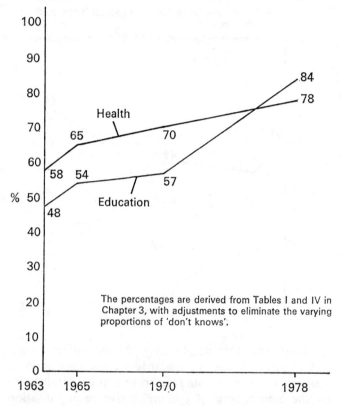

The percentages are derived from Tables I and IV in Chapter 3, with adjustments to eliminate the varying proportions of 'don't knows'.

support for the present system would then appear to vanish altogether within five years. But even if we project the more moderate average rate of increase for option C since 1963 (an annual rate of at least 2%), we would arrive at the astonishing figure of 80% support for individual freedom to contract out by 1988.

COMPARISONS BY OCCUPATIONAL AND
POLITICAL CATEGORIES

As with differences in preferences in health, the only significant variations shown in Table V are all in the directions we would expect: the present system (option A) is favoured by more Labour sympathisers (21%) than Conservative (12%), and freedom to contract out attracts more Conservative (63%) than Labour sympathisers (54%). The most impressive evidence of the widespread discontent with present policies is provided by the finding that only 15% of occupational groups C2DE supported option A in 1978, the identical figure

Table V
Policy for Education: Occupational and Party Differences, 1978

Question 15	(Base: total sample 1,992)				
		Occupational Group		Party Sympathy	
	All	ABC1	C2DE	Con.	Lab.
Policy Option	%	%	%	%	%
A. Keep present system	15	15	15	12	21
B. Concentrate on poor	17	14	19	18	18
C. Allow contracting out	60	63	57	63	54
'Don't know'	8	8	9	7	7

as for the higher ABC1 groups. The assumption that contracting out is of most interest to middle or upper social groups (with their traditional support for public, direct grant and grammar schools) is plainly disproved by Table V, which shows that freedom for individuals to contract out is favoured by as many as 57% of the C2DEs compared with 63% of the ABC1s.

Again, as with health, if we single out Labour supporters as the most likely to defend the present system, the remarkable indication is that in education policy 77% (not counting 'don't knows') would prefer contracting out, either automatically for people not in need (favoured by 19%) *or* by individual discretion (58%). If we exclude the 'don't knows' from the answers of the full sample in 1978, the combined support for both forms of contracting out (options B and C) in education rises to the remarkable proportion of 84% (Table IV and Chart F).

C. GENERAL ATTITUDES TOWARDS TAXES AND WELFARE

It may be objected that, by confining people to expressing their preferences between two among a wider conceivable range of alternative policies in state health and education, we were unduly constraining their choices to more or less formalised, far-reaching reforms of present arrangements. Accordingly, the questionnaire invited attitudes towards two more general but contrasting viewpoints on the relative merits of accepting higher taxes or paying personally for some welfare services. To each of the following statements, people were asked to say whether they agreed/agreed strongly or disagreed/disagreed strongly:

'If I could get better welfare services I would be prepared to pay more for them in higher taxes.'

'I would prefer to have a system of lower taxes and pay for some welfare services myself.'

The answers (summarised in Tables VI and VII) broadly confirm the strong balance of opinion against paying higher taxes—even though it is implicit in the first option that the taxpayer would in return be assured of better services of the kind he personally values (which we have seen the ballot box can never guarantee).

Thus Table VI indicates a decisive majority of people expressing a preference as opposed to paying higher taxes for better services: by 49% against 38% (or by 56% against 44% if we exclude the 13% expressing no preference). The only significant variations among the sub-categories were by political sympathy. Again it may surprise many close observers of the conventional party

Table VI
Would Pay Higher Taxes: 1978

Question 21	(Base: total sample 1,992)				
		Occupational Group		Party Sympathy	
	All	*ABC1*	*C2DE*	*Con.*	*Lab.*
	%	%	%	%	%
Agree strongly	3 ⎫ 38	38	38	34	46
Agree	35 ⎭				
Neutral	13	13	12	10	11
Disagree	40 ⎫ 49	49	51	56	43
Disagree strongly	9 ⎭				

debate that Labour supporters who might be expected to favour more public expenditure, especially on their chosen welfare services, are shown to be almost exactly equally divided: 46% agree with higher taxes and 43% disagree. And perhaps no less significant, the lower occupational groups are as emphatic as the higher groups in not wishing to pay higher taxes even for better welfare services.

Table VII shows a similar picture, with a majority of

52% of the whole sample saying they favoured less taxes with more personal payment and 37% opposing. Excluding the neutrals, the majority is 58% against 42%. The political sub-division shows the expected divergences which are, however, more marked, with 37% of Labour supporters approving lower taxes and 51% disapproving. The analysis by occupational groups reveals a departure from the political pattern that may surprise observers who think in stereotypes

Table VII
Prefer Lower Taxes: 1978

Question 21	(Base: total sample 1,992)				
			Occupational Group		Party Sympathy
	All %		ABC1 %	C2DE %	Con. %	Lab. %
Agree strongly	7 ⎫ 52		62	46	65	37
Agree	45 ⎭					
Neutral	11		10	12	8	12
Disagree	33 ⎫ 37		29	42	27	51
Disagree strongly	4 ⎭					

and too easily assume that Labour views are more or less synonymous with those of the C2DEs. Thus the option of lower taxes is approved by 37% of Labour supporters but by 46% of the C2DEs—more than the 42% who oppose lower taxes. A plausible explanation which is consistent with similar though less marked contrasts elsewhere between class and political attitudes is that the 61% of the total sample expressing a Conservative or Labour sympathy tend to be more paternalistic in favouring state (=political) provision than others who do not identify themselves so readily with either party and may mistrust all politicians.

D. TOLERANCE FOR PRIVATE HEALTH AND EDUCATION

Another option for public policy—short of positively encouraging people to contract out and enabling them through tax refunds to pay directly for some/all welfare services—would be to rely on the gradual encroachment of private choice as the general tax burden is reduced and rising prosperity enables people to pay for education and health insurance out of net income (without a tax refund).

To the obstacle that such people in effect pay twice for the privilege of choice in welfare, the Labour Government has recently gone out of its way to add further discouragements (and to envisage still more impediments—if not outright prohibition) to private education and hospital services. Since the intensification of such policies would increasingly render more difficult moves in the direction of widening choice, we included in the 1978 survey a specific (macro) question on individual attitudes towards *other* people's freedom (as well as their own) to spend their own incomes on private welfare services. The method was to offer an affirmative statement of the view, implicit in the Labour Party's restrictive policy on both services, that people generally should *not* be allowed to pay for private welfare and to invite a graduated (more/less) indication of public support. The statements put to the sample were in the following terms:

A 'People who want to should not be allowed to pay extra for themselves for the health services which they need outside the Health Service.'

B 'People who want to should not be allowed to pay extra to send their children to fee-paying schools.'

To both statements, respondents were asked whether they agreed strongly, agreed, neither agreed nor disagreed, disagreed, or disagreed strongly.

The results (summarised in Table VIII) point to the unmistakable conclusion that there is a massive rejection of the exclusive state monopoly in both health and education services by 80-81% against 13-15%. There were

Table VIII
Prevention of Private Payment?

Question 21	(Base: total sample 1,992)			
	A. *Private Health*		B. *Private Education*	
	All	*Labour*	*All*	*Labour*
	%	%	%	%
Agree strongly	2⎫ 15	4⎫ 20	2⎫ 13	4⎫ 18
Agree	13⎭	16⎭	11⎭	14⎭
Neutral	5	7	5	7
Disagree	55⎫ 80	56⎫ 72	54⎫ 81	56⎫ 75
Disagree strongly	25⎭	16⎭	27⎭	19⎭

no significant variations between the sub-groupings, except for Labour sympathisers, and even their opposition was hardly less overwhelming, only 18-20% agreeing that people 'should not be allowed . . .' against 72-75% disagreeing.

80 PER CENT TOLERANCE OF CHOICE

This picture of a population preponderantly tolerant of, if not necessarily personally inclined to pay for, private welfare services is completely consistent with the preferences expressed on the macro-policy choices which revealed support of 72% (in health) and 77% (in education) for policies requiring or permitting people to contract out of state services (options B and C).

Nor is this picture of 80% tolerance towards payment for private welfare services in any way in conflict with the lower proportions that would accept a voucher for education (51%) or health services (57%) (Chapter 5). In the first place, the maximum voucher offered was two-thirds of the cost of private payment, which would leave the recipient to add one-third from net income. At a higher voucher value, the proportion accepting would clearly rise well above 60%. Secondly, the relatively narrow difference in support for contracting out between the two broad occupational groups suggests that many who have never known anything but state services for themselves and their families favour policies that would keep the door open to private alternatives as an option for themselves in the future as average incomes continue to rise.

Thus all the indications of public attitudes towards alternative directions for policy confirm support for a radical change that would permit individuals freedom to contract out of state education and health services. Nor can the dwindling minority who oppose such a re-direction of policy be cited as a pretext for obstructing a change. Under a system of contracting out by voluntary option (C), they would be left with the individual choice to continue paying taxes for state services. How long they continued to pay taxes for them would depend on what education and medical care they saw other citizens receiving in return for their school fees and insurance premiums. But at least they would be making the decision both without compulsion (which the Welfare State now imposes on them) and with knowledge of possible alternatives (which it prevents them from acquiring).

CHAPTER 4

Ballot-Box or Market-Place?

How can we explain the contrast between the preferences of individuals revealed by our surveys and the policies enforced on them by politicians of all parties in the name of representative democracy? The clue was provided in a recent and remarkable supplement to *The Economist* where Mr Norman Macrae[1] declared:

'Across the English-speaking world, the system of government is breaking down . . . democracy is dying . . .'

His evidence was drawn chiefly from Britain but also from the United States, Canada, South Africa and Australia. In all five countries governments of apparently widely differing political persuasions have taken ever-increasing powers over the economy, yet they seem equally *impotent* to satisfy those they claim to represent by fulfilling the promises on which they had been elected.[2]

THE FOLLY OF CONSENSUS

While the countries Mr Macrae reviewed exhibited marked differences in resources, incomes per head, historical development, cultural, political and social structure, the shared experience to which he attributed

[1] Mr Macrae is Deputy Editor, *The Economist*: 23 December 1978.
[2] This process is trenchantly described by Richard Rose and Guy Peters in *Can Government Go Bankrupt?*, The Macmillan Co., 1979.

their common malaise was the post-war consensus in favour of the cumulative extension of governmental/ bureaucratic control over industry, social welfare, local services, employment and—as an inevitable by-product —over the proportion of national income taken in taxes.

It may seem ungenerous to take Mr Macrae's diagnosis in 1978 as a text to measure the failure of economists to warn politicians sooner against the dangerous path they were treading—all too often with the uncritical support of non-party journals like *The Economist* itself. Yet the politician had his own reasons for acquiescing in or even welcoming collectivist panaceas. The promise of more benefits simultaneously appeared to placate pressure groups and enlarge political power and prestige—at least in the short run until their full costs began to emerge along with the chronic failure of big government. There was less excuse for independent economists. They should have known better, not least because their proper concern is with a more profound analysis than counting votes and a longer time-horizon than the next election.

It is now almost exactly 30 years since D. H. (Sir Dennis) Robertson warned his fellow-economists against the political opportunism that has since threatened to bring economics as formerly the most advanced of the social sciences into the kind of disrepute from which modern sociology has never emerged. In his Presidential Address to the Royal Economic Society[2] entitled 'On Sticking to One's Last', he anticipated the temptation to which many professional economists, especially at his own Cambridge, have since succumbed:

[2] Reprinted in the *Economic Journal,* December 1949.

'I feel sure that if the economist is in too much of a hurry to pose as the complete man—too anxious to show that he is duly sensitive to "the changed temper of the age" and has taken full account of what is "politically and psychologically possible"—he will be in danger of betraying his calling.

Twenty-five years ago it needed some spirit on his part to develop the case for deficit financing as a remedy for trade depression without being prematurely silenced by the argument that it would scare the business man and so do more harm than good. Now the boot is on the other foot, and it takes some spirit to state clearly and fairly the case for wage reduction as a cure for unemployment or an adverse balance of payments, or the case for a curtailment of subsidies and the overhauling of social services as a solvent of inflationary pressure, *without being prematurely silenced by the argument that nowadays the Trade Unions would never stand for such things.* Perhaps they wouldn't; but that is no reason for not following the argument whithersoever it leads . . .

I do not want the economist to mount the pulpit or expect him to fit himself to handle the keys of Heaven and Hell. I want him to be rather brave and rather persistent in hammering in those results achieved within his own domain about which he feels reasonably confident, not too readily reduced to silence by the plea that this, that or the other is ruled out of court by custom, or justice, or the temper of the age.' (*Italics added.*)

BEST USE OF RESOURCES?

Since its foundation in 1957, the Institute of Economic Affairs has deliberately followed Robertson's injunction by inviting its authors to pursue the logic of their analysis without political fear or favour. Economists as citizens are, of course, entitled to their own philosophic predilections about the kind of society they would like to live in. But as scholars they are not concerned with justifying the policies pursued by one or even all of the parties. Their function is to advance understanding of the choices that the ineluctable fact of scarce resources imposes on the community as producers and consumers in the political no less than the economic market.

If the economist's distinctive concern had to be expressed briefly in everyday language it would be along the lines of encouraging the best use of scarce human and material resources. The outcome of a long debate between classical, neo-classical and socialist economists demonstrates that there is no agreement on a more objective assessment of 'best use' than the combined subjective valuations of millions of consumers spending their own money—which enforces economy because no individual's income is ever sufficient to buy all he could wish. Nor has economic theory or practice discovered a better—or less imperfect—mechanism for establishing relative values than in the competitive market where advertised prices—despite persuasion—inform consumers of the opportunity cost of each purchase in terms of the alternative lines of spending that must be sacrificed. (Market imperfections are discussed below.)

The 'best use' of scarce resources is never settled once and for all. It is subject to a continuing process of adjustment in the light of new production possibilities and changing consumer preferences. The further merit of the open competitive market is that it allows a continuing re-assessment of 'best use' based on the maximum knowledge of alternatives that is dispersed widely among the general body of producers and consumers. It is this unplanned, spontaneous process that explains the transformation of consumer markets in domestic equipment, furniture, fashion gear, colour photography, frozen foods, hi-fi, cars, caravans, pocket calculators, foreign travel and holidays.

THE CASE FOR GOVERNMENT . . .

In principle, the economic market-place provides a perfect form of democratic selection. It has been likened to a perpetual referendum in which customers vote every day with their money for the widest possible choice between the offerings of competing suppliers. It resolves the issue of 'best use' on the demand side by encouraging consumers to extract the maximum value from their limited spending power, and on the supply side by requiring competing producers to offer what the customer wants at the lowest price.

In practice there are a number of difficulties with the economic market. The most obvious is that voting power depends on incomes which are not only unequal but leave some families with insufficient money to buy the goods and services generally considered a minimum for civilised existence. Another is that some goods and services—from defence to law enforcement—cannot be supplied by competing producers but must be organised collectively. And even where private enterprise does operate, imperfections can arise from monopoly elements, consumer ignorance and the 'spillover' effects of private transactions on third parties. Such possible sources of 'market failure' have long been understood to require intervention by government, going back to the Elizabethan Poor Law and justices of the peace, the even earlier royal ordinance, and the 19th-century laws on public health, property and nuisance, restraint of trade, merchandise marks, joint stock companies, purity of food, and many more.

There is wide scope for argument where the precise boundary should be drawn between collective control or provision by government agencies, on the one hand, and competitive supply or tendering by private producers, on the other. What about roads, street lighting, docks, parks, police, libraries, swimming pools, sports facilities, postal services, refuse removal, housing, pensions and—coming to the chief services studied in this report—health and education? For most of these services, collective supply is not inevitable, as is shown by the continued existence of competing docks, leisure facilities, private security services, builders, insurance companies—to say nothing of competing private hospitals and schools.

It is true that where collective provision is not *required* by the indivisible nature of the service, it may still be *thought desirable* as a way of enforcing a common or minimum standard of quality or safety. Yet experience with goods and services as varied as food, aircraft, clothing, hire purchase, third party insurance, housing, medicine and schooling demonstrates that standards can be prescribed for producers or consumers and enforced by public inspection without collective provision. At the same time, we should be on guard against pushing standards too high so that they raise costs, exclude competition and deny consumers the freedom to choose between higher price and lower (but acceptable) quality.

Economists have devoted much theoretical ingenuity to exposing plausible imperfections of the market due to restrictions on competition or the social costs of private transactions, which have too often provided politicians with a pretext to impose far-reaching government control, subsidisation or outright nationalisation. The twin fallacies concealed behind most of this theorising have been, first, the failure to take account of the practical imperfections of government 'remedy' and, secondly, the refusal to see that many defects are due to acts of omission and commission by government in failing to incorporate the appropriate checks and balances in the legal framework which necessarily surrounds the operation of markets. In simple terms, most restrictions on or distortions of competition stem from government action or inaction; and, even where they do not, the original imperfection is often made worse by government monopolisation, regulation or other well-intended interference.

. . . BEING KEPT TO A MINIMUM

Even where, for example in consumer protection, a realistic comparison of imperfect markets with imperfect government may show a narrow balance in favour of more state intervention, there are increasingly strong economic and political reasons for refraining from burdening politicians with additional functions. The main economic reason follows from the limited time and talents available to government: the more tasks it undertakes, the less effectively can even the best administration and bureaucracy be expected to discharge any of them, including those duties which only government can perform and on which depend the efficient operation of the remaining private sector. This overburdening is the central cause of Mr Macrae's discovery that 'the system of government is breaking down'. The main political reason for curbing the power of government follows from the unavoidable limitations of the democratic electoral process: the more tasks politicians take on, the less can citizens make their wishes effective through voting.

Compared with the sovereign consumer in competitive markets, what sovereignty does the voter exercise through the ballot-box? In place of the daily choice between myriad suppliers, the voter has a single option between two or three political parties at elections every four or five years. Instead of the consumer's freedom to shop around and buy items of varying brands from differing outlets on a pick-and-choose, *à la carte* basis, the citizen must cast his one vote for a single political supplier and swallow the entire manifesto package on a *table d'hôte*, take-it-or-leave-it basis for years on end. Where the commercial firm must accurately label his products and publish their prices, all political parties regularly promise 'free' services without revealing the cost that will be exacted through all kinds of taxes. While commercial advertisers are prohibited from falsely describing their goods or those of their competitors, most political salesmen think nothing of bidding for votes with half-truths, quarter-truths, and outright untruths. Recent elections furnish ample examples, especially on welfare and tax policy.

Above all, the economic market is superior to the political ballot-box in its ability to cater sensitively for minorities on an exact measure of proportional representation. Small groups of consumers with unusual needs or preferences can invariably find a supplier to meet their distinctive requirements at a price. Yet for all the discussion of electoral reform, there is no conceivable change in the voting system that could prevent a government backed by 51 per cent of the electorate from enforcing its will on the other 49 per cent. Where the ballot-box leads to massive coercion of minorities (and even of majorities), the market maximises consent between willing buyers and willing sellers.

For public goods and services that have to be supplied collectively[3] through the machinery of political democracy, there is no practical alternative to the choice-distorting and choice-denying crudity of the ballot-box, leavened perhaps occasionally by a referendum on single issues. Compared, however, with the perpetual referendum of the competitive market, the machinery of political democracy is so far inferior as to establish a strong presumption against using it for any goods and services which can be supplied in response to consumer demand expressed through competitive markets.

Even if governments were models of rectitude and efficiency in implementing their promises, there remains the simple democratic objection to enlarging their functions. The more decisions politicians take, supposedly on our behalf, the less effective is a single vote in expressing approval or disapproval for any particular policy. The value of the vote is, in effect, diluted by being spread over a larger number of issues. Where the market invites the consumer to give case-by-case consent for each separate line of expenditure, 'government by consent' requires the citizen to approve the complete

---

[3] What makes national defence or clean air a 'public good' is not that either is essential so much as that, if they are supplied to some people in an area, the presumed benefit is enjoyed by everyone, whether they would pay for it or not. Hence governments have to provide public goods and finance the cost from compulsory taxation.

range of prospective state spending proposed by one or other party, or to abstain and have it forced upon him.

It is hardly conceivable that any voter supports every policy put forward by his chosen party, yet its leaders will nevertheless claim a binding mandate for every line of small print in their manifesto. Returning to the economist's concern with the way scarce resources are used, and accepting consumer preferences as the most widely agreed measure of 'best use', we can see that a single vote at quinquennial elections provides no assurance that the larger half of national income now disposed of by a government elected by less than 30 per cent of all voters yields anything like the satisfaction generated by the smaller half which consumers spend for themselves in competitive markets. The sober truth lurking behind the fine rhetoric about democracy is that a régime of unlimited government makes it impossible to claim that any specific policy is democratic in the sense of representing the preference of a majority of voters.

GOVERNMENT VERSUS MARKET FORCES

An insecure foundation for much government intervention is the assumption that by passing laws politicians can impose their will on what they like to scorn as 'blind market forces'. The classic refutation of this superficial view was set out more than half a century ago by the Austrian economist Böhm-Bawerk in *Power or Economic Law?*,[4] which argued that intervention in the market could distort but not supplant the operation of

---

[4] First published in German in 1914 and translated in *Shorter Classics of Eugen von Böhm-Bawerk*, Libertarian Press, USA, 1961.

the fundamental law of supply and demand which, for example,

> 'had been observed to triumph over the attempts of powerful governments to render bread cheap in lean years by means of "unnatural" price regulation, or to confer upon bad money the purchasing power of good money'.

'Blind market forces' are nothing more than the spontaneous outcome of individuals making decisions as buyers and sellers in the light of the prices of alternative goods and services. Market prices emerge as the balancing factor between the two flows of competing supplies and consumer choices. In Böhm-Bawerk's succinct formulation:

> 'price is fixed at the intersection of supply and demand, at that point where equal quantities are offered and taken'.

If governments seek to regulate any one of the variables, it is folly to assume the others will obligingly remain unchanged. The unhappy results of well-intentioned social policies that ignore this economic truism are most dramatically seen in the 60-year-long history of British rent controls which sought to help tenants by holding down the price of rented accommodation. The aim of political 'control' was abundance of cheap housing; the outcome of 'economic law' was that the supply of housing to let was reduced and the cost of uncontrolled housing was driven still higher.[5] In formal economic terms: where the market price rations scarce resources among competing uses, the suppression or subsidisation of price converts scarcity into chronic shortage by expanding demand and constricting supply.

[5] Norman Macrae, *To Let?*, Hobart Paper 2, IEA, 1960; *Verdict on Rent Control*, IEA Readings No. 7, IEA, 1972.

This basic market analysis is sufficient to provide an explanation of the mounting complaints about shortages throughout the welfare sectors of education and medical care since governments embarked on their post-war ambition to bring 'the best standards to everyone'[6] without what economically illiterate sociologists like to call the 'barrier' of price. There were a number of false hopes underlying this apparently idealistic surge of welfare collectivism, not least Beveridge's claim that improved health care (and Lord Vaizey's later claim[7] that more education) could yield a high return and even cover its cost through increased production and the prize of sustained economic growth. But the central fallacy[8] was in assuming that a fixed quantum of schools, teachers, doctors, nurses, hospitals and equipment would guarantee universal access to 'the best' education and medical care. In economists' jargon, it assumed demand was 'inelastic' and would therefore not increase if price was abolished or artificially reduced.

It was as mistaken as it would be to suppose government could undertake to supply essential food free of charge without the certainty that demand would always run ahead of available supplies, not least for the best cuts of meat, freshest vegetables and choicest pastries. No competent economist should be surprised that expenditure on social services has since 1950 grown

---

[6] The 1944 Coalition White Paper spoke of ensuring that 'every man, woman and child can rely on getting . . . the best medical and other facilities . . . [irrespective of] whether they can pay for them or of any other factor irrelevant to the real need . . .'

[7] *The Economics of Education,* Faber & Faber, 1962.

[8] J. M. Buchanan, *Inconsistencies of the National Health Service*, Occasional Paper 7, IEA, 1965.

from around 15 per cent to above 25 per cent of the national income without ushering in the universal abundance that was to have replaced the old régime of economic scarcity.

MORE . . . OR LESS WELFARE?

Politicians easily salve their consciences by falling back on the argument that at least government provision ensures more resources are devoted to welfare than if consumers were required to pay the market prices. But even for the poorest consumers this contention would be true only on the gratuitous assumption that no alternative policy was available to remedy their poverty. The best that can be said for the 'universalist' policy of free services is that it operates like a blunderbuss: by scattering benefits widely it aims to miss no-one who may be in need of them. Yet, despite the mischievous and wilful obfuscation about dislike of 'means tests', a more efficient method of raising minimum standards is available through a 'selective' policy of topping-up low incomes. A system of reverse income tax[9] would enable everyone to buy the minimum of welfare services—along with food, clothing and domestic supplies—through the more sensitively democratic mechanism of the competitive market.

But however relative the prevailing conception of 'poverty' in an advanced economy, it must be assumed to embrace only a minority of the population. Even if 'free' services enabled them to consume more welfare than previously, should we assume the same to be true

[9] Colin Clark, *Poverty before Politics,* Hobart Paper 73, IEA, 1977; IEA Study Group, *Policy for Poverty,* Research Monograph 20, IEA, 1970.

of the better-off majority? The rhetoric of 'free benefits' appears to have misled many, through the 'fallacy of composition', into believing that 'the state' is somehow able to devote more resources to welfare than are available to all the individuals comprising it. This illusion of 'something for nothing' was finally pricked by the Central Statistical Office. Since the early 1960s it has published a regular series of tables comparing for families of varying size and income the benefits derived from 'free' and subsidised welfare services on the one hand, with the family cost in rates, National Insurance and all other taxes. The consistent lesson of these statistics (examined more closely in Chapter 7) is that millions of families with incomes significantly below the average regularly pay more in taxes than the combined value of all the 'free' services provided for them by the pretended benevolence of the Welfare State.

In short, despite all the talk about the compassion of politicians and the boon of the Welfare State, it was demonstrated that the majority of people were more than paying their own way in welfare. Indeed, if we allow that bureaucratic-monopoly provision will be less efficient and more costly than the same services supplied in competitive markets, we may conclude that consumers were paying dear for 'free' services. And if they were paying their way, what was left of the case for denying them the range of choice in all aspects of education and medical care that only the referendum of the market could provide? The principal effect of collective welfare services can now be seen as taxing away so much of the income of most families that they are reduced to dependence upon state services, *whether satisfied with them or not*. The continued use of state services cannot be taken as evidence of satisfaction since few can afford to pay from their heavily taxed income the cost of opting for private education or health insurance. In other words, choice of welfare in the market would require double payment: the tax-payer is charged for the 'free' state services, whether he wants them or not, and would have to pay all over again for the private alternative in the market. Not least of the disservices inflicted by state welfare has been to buttress the near-monopolies in education and medical care by inhibiting the growth of competing, cost-effective private services.

CHOICE IN WELFARE

At least since the early 1960s, discontent with the inadequacies of state education and medical care has suggested to perceptive observers that increasing num-bers of families might like to devote part of their rising incomes to getting more of what they want in welfare. The dilemma was bravely expressed by Douglas (now Lord) Houghton in 1967 shortly after resigning as a senior Minister in the Wilson Government with responsibility for trying to co-ordinate social policy:

> 'While people would be willing to pay for better services for themselves, they may not be willing to pay more in taxes as a kind of insurance premium which may bear no relation to the services actually received.'[10]

The significance of this observation, which can be matched by quotations from other social democrats in

[10] *Paying for the Social Services,* Occasional Paper 16, IEA, 1967 (2nd Edition, 1968).

the Labour Party,[11] is that it directs attention to the way in which the dependence of welfare on finance extracted from citizens as taxpayers may not increase but *reduce* the resources devoted to education and medical care by frustrating individual and family choice. Such a possibility is borne out by evidence from other countries where mixed systems of state and private welfare show a higher proportion of rising incomes attracted into medical care than in the National Health Service.

Since economists have always been alert to the scope for monopoly to exclude alternatives and divert scarce resources away from their best use, it is remarkable that there has not been more scepticism about the political claims made by all parties for near-monopoly provision of tax-financed welfare services. From the independent vantage point of the Institute of Economic Affairs—holding no brief for any party—it was clear from the outset that the machinery of political elections, operating within the limits of a Fabian-Beveridge consensus, did not and could not reflect the evidently wide spectrum of individual and family preferences on welfare services that took such a large slice of national resources. Our hypothesis from observation of other markets was that people would prefer policies in welfare that permitted freer choice of the form and amount of education and medical care. So long as politicians obstruct experimentation with policies that would offer alternative services and invite each family to vote with its own money, social scientists must make the most of substitute voting mechanisms which improve on the

[11] Notably in Richard Crossman's White Paper on *National Superannuation* (Cmnd. 3883, January 1969) and in speeches by Brian Walden when a Labour MP.

blind man's buff of the ballot-box though they fall short of the refined referendum of the competitive market-place.

We pass on to the findings of such substitute voting mechanisms.

CHAPTER 5

Your Choice between State and Market Welfare

A fundamental difference between the IEA approach and the approach in other social surveys until the 1960s must be emphasised if the significance of our approach —which sought not general opinions or attitudes in vacuo but choices between alternatives clearly labelled with price-tags—is to be understood. To our knowledge these macro-micro tests had not been systematically applied in other surveys since the war designed to learn the state of public opinion about the Welfare State, or its separate parts.[1] Since they generally omitted price, they seemed, not surprisingly, to find a large measure— sometimes 80% or 90%—of approval, acceptance, support or acclaim. Such 'price-less' surveys continued in the 1960s, and are not unknown today.

In 1957, for example, a Political and Economic Planning (PEP) price-less inquiry found general satisfaction with the National Health Service. In 1962 Research Services Limited asked (for the Institute of Community Studies): 'Would you say you were for or against the Welfare State?'; not surprisingly 94% were 'for' and not 'against'. In 1964 Research Services asked (for the Association of the British Pharmaceutical

---

[1] The other surveys till the mid-1960s are reviewed in A. Seldon and H. Gray, *Universal or Selective Social Benefits?*, Research Monograph 8, IEA, 1967.

Industry): 'Do you think . . . the NHS is . . . working reasonably well or not?'; 88% replied, kindly and compassionately, 'Yes'. Politicians who resisted, or did not relish, change, and bureaucrats whose jobs depended on the *status quo*, said nothing to question these priceless and therefore worthless statistics. No economist who understands market pricing—in the capitalist West or the Communist East—would make this mistake.

(These price-less surveys continue: the latest seems to have been in November 1978 when NOP asked 'How satisfied are you with the care you get at present from the National Health Service?' 45% replied 'very satisfied', 39% 'fairly satisfied'. The total 'satisfaction' at 84% does not seem to have changed since the 1950s, but is no more significant as a measure of public preference.)

To us as economists it was plain that these surveys were fundamentally flawed, and that their findings of almost universal approval of state health or welfare services were misleading students of social policy, politicians and the public.

THERE AIN'T NO SUCH THING AS 'WANT'
WITHOUT PRICE

Preferences between alternative satisfactions, the desire or, in economic language, the 'demand' for one product or service rather than another, cannot be decided except in terms of their relative prices. There ain't no such thing as the demand for anything except related to its price.[2] It is obvious that an individual will 'want', 'prefer', 'demand' more of a service the lower its price,

---

[2] Professor Milton Friedman has made effective use of the Cockney-phrased economic aphorism 'There ain't no such
[*Continued on page 81*]

and less the higher its price. This economic 'law of demand' holds because the price measures the value of the alternatives that have to be sacrificed or lost in buying something. The lower the price, the less the sacrifice of other things, and the more will be 'demanded'. If the price is astronomic, demand may be nil; if price is nil, demand may be astronomic. To speak of 'demand', or 'want', or 'preference' without linking it to a price is meaningless. And the same is true of supply. But it is a common mistake made in politics, by interviewers on TV and radio, and in the press. Although the relationship is obvious once explained, even some economists tend to forget it.

This is also fundamentally why economic systems with central planners who try to allocate resources to the numerous possible alternative uses without being guided by price sooner or later run into confusion and chaos; and why the Communist governments in Hungary, Poland,[3] Yugoslavia and Russia have been trying to restore a pricing—or 'market'—system to bring some order and reason into their 'planning'. The

[*Continued from page 80*]

    thing as a free lunch' (in *There's No Such Thing as a Free Lunch,* Open Court Publishing, La Salle, Ill., 1970, 2nd edn. with additional material published as *An Economist's Protest,* Thomas Horton, Glen Ridge, N.J., 1972). It was also adroitly deployed by Professor E. D. Dolan in the book he entitled *TANSTAAFL* (Holt, Reinhart & Winston, New York, 1971). Professor Dolan says the originator was Robert Heinlein in *The Moon is a Harsh Mistress,* 1966.

[3] An example of this thinking is by Professor Witold Trzeciakowski, Chairman of the Polish Foreign Trade Research Institute, in *Systems of Indirect Management in a Planned Economy,* University of Lodz, 1973: by 'indirect' (in contrast to direct state-controlled) management is meant maximising profit in a centrally planned system that tries to use prices.

prices they create may be faulty, or artificial, but without them blind planners are leading blindfolded citizens.

PRICE IN ASSESSING PUBLIC PREFERENCES

Economists saw that the fundamental importance of the IEA surveys in 1963 and 1965 was that they had introduced price into studies of public preferences. The first was Professor Mark Blaug, the noted historian of economic thought, who wrote in 1967:

> 'Economists will recognise immediately that the [*Choice in Welfare*] inquiry in effect elicited information about the slope of the demand schedule [for education] . . .'[4]

Professor Blaug added that the 'taste' for education 'is itself a function of the education of parents'. This is true, as confirmed by the 1978 inquiry, which asked and analysed the replies from people not only indirectly by socio-economic group, which reflects the extent of education, but more directly by extent (or length) of education —up to 16 years and over 16 (p. 96). Professor Jack Wiseman, also in 1967, emphasised that field studies on social policies must discover opinion about possible alternatives to current practices in terms of their (relative) prices.[5]

Although it is not possible to build individual prices into questions on macro-policies, our surveys since 1963 made it clear that the choice was between policies that

---

[4] *Education: A Framework for Choice*, Readings No. 1, IEA, 1967 (2nd Edition, 1970). A demand 'schedule' is simply a list that relates the amount demanded at each price, so that, if the price of apples or shirts or education or medicine goes down, the demand invariably goes up, more or less according to its 'elasticity'.

[5] *New Society*, 2 November 1967.

required taxes as means of payment to government for state services and the alternative of paying directly by prices for private welfare in the market. People were therefore asked not for opinions or preferences (wants, demands) *in vacuo* but in clear relation to the two alternative means of payment—prices or taxes. It is the IEA pricing techniques that, seven years after 1963, drew the admission from Mr Timothy Raison in 1970 that the surveys published in his journal *New Society* in 1967 had been defective, and that only the price-related IEA surveys were significant:

'This [*New Society*] survey was an attitude survey—and perfectly valid as such. But this did not necessarily mean that it was wholly valuable as a policy-making aid. Even where it is based on actual experience, it only tells us what people think about what is—*not about what might be,* which is after all what politics is largely about.'

'. . . the crucial question of what research can or cannot do [is] to help us in the *evaluation of alternatives*—the "would you be prepared to *pay* such-and-such in order to receive such-and-such" type of question with which the IEA has experimented. One must, in other words, talk about costs as well as about [the quantity of] services.'[6] (*Our italics.*)

THE PRICE-LESS POLITICIANS

Price is thus indispensable to understanding, and its absence causes politicians and others, knowingly or unknowingly, to mislead the public. They sometimes claim that the public wants both lower taxes and better (or at least not worse) public services. The implication

[6] *Social Policy and Social Research,* Paper delivered to a market research conference, 1974.

is that it is fruitless to ask the public questions on taxes and 'public' services, because the public wants incompatible objects.

If price is excluded, the politicians are right: people would want inordinate public services if they were 'free', and probably nil taxes if public services did not have to be paid for in other ways. To put it even more simply: 'If it's free, put me down for two'. But it is the politicians who are confused. They persistently fail to put the alternatives to the public correctly. To adapt the common parlance: if you ask unanswerable questions, you receive contradictory answers. The questions must include the element of price. They should run:

'Do you want lower taxes *at the price of paying for services in other ways*?'

'Do you want better public services (or avoid deteriorating services) *at the price of higher taxes*?'

If these alternatives are asked in terms of their prices, the public does not indicate incompatible opinion, as their replies to the IEA field inquiries demonstrate. Although government does not ask priced questions, the IEA surveys indicate that the British are capable of making choices logically and consistently. It is unconvincing to maintain, and impossible to accept, that people who understand they must pay for the elemental essentials of food, clothing and shelter are incapable of understanding that they must pay for education and medicine (or housing and pensions). The reason for their initial difficulty is not an innate inability to understand that desirable services require payment, but the concealment of this truth by the suppression of price in the Welfare State.

A. EDUCATION

THE METHOD OF ASSESSING MICRO-CHOICE

To discover the preferences between (tax-paid) state education and (fee-paid) private education, we used the device of the voucher. To see how the desire (preference, demand) for a choice varied with its price, all parents with children of school age were asked how they would respond to a voucher with two values. More values would have yielded more points on the demand 'schedule', but for simplicity this new kind of inquiry was begun with two values, which were then repeated in the later surveys for continuity. Whatever the limitations of measuring choice or demand by this method, they were constant in all the field surveys, which thus yield a broad indication of the probable trend in the demand for choice.

The value of the voucher was related to the estimated cost of statutory (to 16 years) state secondary schooling: it could not be obtained for 1963, but was £150 in 1965, £225 in 1970, £450 in 1978. (Sixth form costs are higher: in 1978 nearer £600.) The parents were asked if they would take the voucher valued at $\frac{1}{3}$ or $\frac{2}{3}$ of the average state school cost, and add the balance of $\frac{2}{3}$ or $\frac{1}{3}$ to pay fees for private education, and therefore, by implication, if they would prefer to stay with state education.

It was implied that private schooling could be obtained for such a sum: private school fees have varied widely, below as well as much above state school costs. (The range is indicated at page 88.) Where fees are higher, the topping-up will be more; where they are lower, the topping-up will be less. Direct comparison between state costs and private fees is difficult because the schools differ, in teaching methods, curricula, etc., not least in responsiveness to parents' wishes or preferences. The final choice would be increasingly left to parents. But it is probable that the increasing use of the voucher, and the new competition it would introduce, would tend to reduce costs and fees because schools would become increasingly cost-conscious (a senior state school official in Australia said to one of the authors: 'It is true: the lights are not switched off as promptly as they are in private schools').*

New technology such as TV would also reduce costs by making possible education in small groups by tutors, or at home, or in schools run by teacher co-operatives, whose administrative, overhead and other costs would tend to be less than those of formal education by classes in buildings called schools. A return of taxes, by voucher or cash, could thus in time be used to pay for new, cheaper, and probably better forms of education such as are being decided in 'alternative' schools by parents in Britain (and abroad) who are dissatisfied with state education.

SAVE THE STATE SCHOOLS BY VOUCHERS?

Professor Stephen D. Sugarman, a lawyer at the University of California, Berkeley, has argued that the voucher is desirable in the USA in order to save the state schools from the private schools, which are increasingly drawing pupils away from them. The important aspect of his opinion is that the conclusion for policy is the opposite from that drawn by supporters of state education in Britain, who argue that the voucher

*'The Potential Market for Education with Choice' is outlined in the panel on pp. 88-9, and in Appendix E.

should therefore be obstructed. Professor Sugarman draws the opposite conclusion that it should be encouraged and introduced.

It is significant that some former supporters of conventional state education, such as Dr Eric Midwinter, Chairman of the Advisory Centre for Education (ACE), are increasingly apprehensive of the power of teachers, teachers' unions and education bureaucrats to thwart parents. They have been arguing not only the case for giving parents a stronger voice within state schools through the familiar representative machinery of parent/ teacher associations, but also, and more significantly, for a new form of self-help by parents in creating schools outside the institutionalised state education system. Their aspiration is to obtain state finance for such quasi-independent schools, of which there is an example in Denmark. But they have not solved three difficulties: first, whether schools would retain parental control if they are state-financed; second, that the 'voice' of the articulate middle-class parent would remain stronger than that of the working-class parent; third, that voices are sure to be heard only when their owners can escape through 'exits', such as a device like the voucher would make possible.

EDUCATION VOUCHERS: SURVEY RESULTS

To inform the respondents of the cost of (day secondary) education they were asked in the 1978 survey whether they would add $\frac{2}{3}$ of the fee (£300) to a voucher valued at $\frac{1}{3}$ of school costs (estimated at £450 a year in 1978), and whether they would add a third (£150) to a voucher worth $\frac{2}{3}$ of school costs.

[Continued on page 90]

THE POTENTIAL MARKET FOR EDUCATION WITH CHOICE

The 51% of parents with children up to 18 who said in 1978 they would 'top up' a $\frac{2}{3}$-value voucher worth £300 numbered probably over 5 million. They would find a small market of private ('public') schools (with around 195,000 day places) that would grow gradually into a mixture of state and private schools.

●   Initially the £450 would require further topping up for most public schools with day fees of £600 to £1,200 a year, although there may be some private schools with lower fees. (Lists of 'public' schools, curricula and other details, fees, etc, are supplied by the Independent Schools Information Service: address at Appendix E.)

●   If the voucher after age 15-16 were raised to $\frac{2}{3}$ of state VIth form costs (£600), it would rise from £300 to £400.

●   State costs and private fees cannot be equated closely because the products differ. The higher fees for the private school cover elements that may make it better value for money than the state school:
- *choice of school*
- *more personal teaching for the exceptional pupil*
- *more disciplined study*
- *more varied non-academic activities*
- *continuous schooling from 11/13 to 18/19*
- *scope for emphasis on religion*
- *a wide range of size of schools*
- *small classes*
- *more single-sex schooling for boys or girls if preferred*
- *close liaison between home and school*
- *freedom from political influence*
- *easy access to Heads and staff*
- *an equal voice for parents of all social classes*
- *unrestricted exit*
- *consumer authority through direct payment.*

III

● Eventually costs and fees would be increasingly disciplined by competition between private and state schools.

● State schools would improve if the shift to private schools grew significantly; all schools would become more cost-conscious and economic in using resources.

● Costs would be contained, and could be reduced, as new forms of schools with low overhead costs were formed to provide for voucher parents/pupils. (Information from the Association for Independent Education and Education Otherwise–Appendix E.) Vouchers could also be used for teacher co-operative or darent-organised schools or schools at home (since education is a matter of content, not of the building in which it takes place).

● Private schools sometimes reduce the costs to parents by bursaries and scholarships.

● Schools would become more diversified and special-ised as they responded to voucher parents with individual children's requirements and with increasing experience in judging schools.

● Widening use of vouchers would encourage the development of new methods of financing the topping up through life assurance, spreading the sums over longer than the school years, and others.

*   *   *

The Tolerated Markets in Education and Medicine
(Figures used for Chart, p.ii)

	Education (% of children of school age at private schools)	Medicine (% of population insured privately)
	%	%
1963	6·4	2·4
1965	5·9	2·8
1970	4·8	3·6
1978	4·2	4·1

IIIIIIIIIIIIIIIIIIIIIIIIIIIIIIIIIIIIIIIIIIIIIIIIIIIIIIIIIIIIIIIIIIIIIIIIIIIIIIIIIIIIIIIIIIIIIIIIIIIIIII

The readiness of men in the 1978 sample to add to the voucher showed a large increase in the 13 years since 1965 (Table I), although the rate of increase was slower after 1970. (Men are initially compared with earlier surveys which were confined to men; but women in 1978 did not differ and are also shown.)

In the 1963 and 1965 surveys the sample was confined to fathers with children of school age as the working heads of households who made the decisions and choices we were investigating. Following suggestions that women should have been included,[7] a check sample of 200 women was added in the 1970 survey to see if they differed from the men, in particular whether they were any less in favour of a choice in welfare. They were not. In the 1978 survey a full statistical complement of mothers was included in the sample from the outset. Broadly their choices did not differ very markedly from those of fathers. For the same reason (that we were studying family decision-makers) the sample in all four surveys since 1963 has excluded people over 65 as no longer directly or substantially concerned with decisions on paying for education, health services and pensions.

The school voucher questions in 1978 were:

'If the state gave you £150 a year for each child aged 11 or more which could only be spent on secondary education—and you would probably have to pay another £300 yourself to make up the fees—do you think you would accept that offer or not?'

[7] Not all critics agreed. Professor Gordon Forsyth wrote in his appraisal of the health voucher results: 'associated surveys suggest that decisions affecting the choice of welfare are indeed taken by husbands and not wives'. (*Doctors and State Medicine*, Pitman Medical Publishing Co., 1967, 2nd Edition, 1973.)

Table I
Suppressed Demand for Choice in Education, 1963-1978

Proportion of male heads of households* who would add to school vouchers to pay annual day fees (with women in 1978)

	1963† men 1,187 %	1965† men 1,218 %	1970† men 1,309 %	1978 men 602 %	1978 women 372 %
Base					
Would add ⅔ to ⅓-value voucher	10‡ } 36 26#	15	27	29	30
Would add ⅓ to ⅔-value voucher	25‡ } 46 21#	30	43	51	52

*with children of school age under 19 years.
†excludes the small proportion who intended to pay for private education.
‡'Very interested'.
#'Interested'.

'And what if the offer were £300 so that you might have to add only another £150; do you think you would accept that offer or not?'

In 1965, 1970 and 1978 vouchers of two values were used to see if the responses followed the 'law of demand' that the lower the price, the higher the demand.

The 1963 results are not strictly comparable with those in the subsequent surveys. In 1963 the voucher was described as 'half' and 'most' of (day) school fees and respondents were asked if they were 'very interested' and 'interested'. Families would have to add the difference between the full fees and 'most'. In the later surveys the values of the vouchers were stated in precise figures representing one-third and two-thirds of fees and the sample was told the estimated fees for day schools and asked more specifically if they would 'accept' them and pay the difference.

Table I shows that for the first time in 1978 the proportion who would add to the voucher worth $\frac{2}{3}$ of fees rose to more than one-half. If political democracy regards a majority as the justification for policy to be applied at all, this finding should be regarded by politicians who appeal to simple majorities as validating a policy of returning two-thirds of school fees to parents and allowing them to add the remaining one-third to pay towards the cost of schools of their choice. If the value of the voucher were $\frac{3}{4}$, $\frac{7}{8}$, or the whole of school fees, the proportion wishing to 'accept' it to exercise choice of school would be higher than 51% and might have reached 60%, 70%, 80%, 90% or 100%. If the voucher covered the whole of the fees, as in the projected experiment in Kent, all parents might wish to use it rather than accept the state school, at least initially until state schools improved, since the voucher makes all schools partly or wholly 'free' but largely removes the disadvantage of political control or administrative discretion. The exceptions might be parents prepared to forego choice for their children in order to act on their belief that all children should attend comprehensive schools.

In 1978 9% said 'don't know'. If they are excluded, as they would be in a referendum vote on a single issue, the 51% rises to 56% of the 'votes' cast.

SEX, AGE, OCCUPATIONAL GROUPS

There was little or no difference in the 1978 figures for men and women for $\frac{2}{3}$ voucher acceptances (51%, 52%), or for younger and older people (16 to 34 years, 50%; 35 to 65 years, 52%).

There was a difference in the demand for choice in education as measured by acceptance of the $\frac{2}{3}$-value voucher between the occupational groups: 56% of the ABC1 group and 48% of the C2DE group in 1978 (Table II). This difference may seem to indicate, not unexpectedly, that the higher the income the easier it is to add £150 to a $\frac{2}{3}$-value voucher to pay the full fees. An implication for policy is that, if it were desired to put a voucher worth less than full fees within the reach of lower-income parents, it could be accompanied by a second voucher to make up for lower incomes. This principle was applied in the compensatory voucher in the 1972-1977 Alum Rock (California) experiment. (There are also other methods of varying the value of the voucher inversely with income: Ch. 8.)

The difference between the two occupational groups is of special interest for the student of family preferences.

The average income in the ABC1 group was probably well over twice that in the C2DE group, yet compared with the 56% among the higher-paid occupations nearly half of the lower-paid group, 48%, were prepared to add £150 a year to the ⅔ voucher for the new power of choice it would give them. What is at first surprising is that only 56% of the higher-income groups opted for the ⅔ voucher. Although middle-income and more monied groups buy choice by paying fees to private schools or by moving to higher-cost homes in middle-class districts with state schools more responsive to parents, some of the more articulate, activist or leisured may find they can help their children by arguing with state school head teachers, officials or politicians without additional payment in private fees or housing costs.

The 48% suggests that the less monied are almost as ready to make financial sacrifices for their children as the more monied. Since the £150 would come out of less well-filled pockets, they may be *more* ready. (Average earnings of the C2s ('skilled working-class') were around £4,000 in 1978, of the Ds and Es less, or much less.) It has always been an unproven reflection on 'the working-classes' that they cared less for their children than did 'the rich'. Perhaps one reason is that social scientists have not used the required tools in discovering the preferences concealed by the layers and decades of the Welfare State.

Although a century of expanding state education has progressively weakened the faculties of judgement and discrimination required in making choices in education, the urge of parents to do the best for their children seems to lie not far below the surface. Policies designed to liberate it might soon find ready response, because the human urge to exercise choice has been nurtured by the experience that markets in food, clothing and other family requirements respond to it, especially as it is progressively strengthened by rising incomes. The rise in incomes would also have been faster had the Welfare State not weakened incentives to produce and depressed the rate of economic growth in Britain.

POLITICAL SYMPATHY

These inferences are strengthened by the surprisingly moderate difference in the responses from Labour-inclined and Conservative-inclined respondents. That

Table II
Suppressed Demand for Choice in Education, 1978:
by Sub-Groups
Questions 16 and 17

Base: Parents with children up to 18: 974 (49% of total sample)

| | Occupational group | | Political sympathy | | Education | |
	ABC1	C2DE	Con.	Lab.	up to 16	over 16
	%	%	%	%	%	%
Would add to $\frac{1}{3}$-value voucher	37	25	38	24	27	42
Would add to $\frac{2}{3}$-value voucher	56	48	60	46	49	60

60% of Conservatives (64% excluding the 6% 'don't knows') would take the two-thirds value voucher is not unexpected. What is more surprising is that almost one in two, or 46%(50% excluding the 8% 'don't knows'), of Labour-inclined heads of families said they would do likewise (Table II).

This result—and the corresponding figures for the health vouchers (pp. 101 *et seq.*)—is for policy-makers in all parties attached to established policies perhaps among the least expected and perhaps most disturbing in the survey. They seem to indicate clear rejection of government in the two main services created by it to raise the lowly, which Mr James Callaghan and others periodically insist is the major domestic purpose or effect of the public/social services.

EDUCATION OF PARENTS AND CHILDREN

Further evidence that rising incomes may continue to strengthen the demand for choice is indicated by the response to the $\frac{2}{3}$ voucher from the two groups according to the degree (length) of education. Compared with the 49% of people prepared to take the $\frac{2}{3}$-value voucher who had themselves left school up to the age of 16, there were no less than 60% of people who had stayed at school to 18 or proceeded to further or higher education. As more people will have had extended education beyond the age of 16 in the next 10 years than in the last 10 or 20, it is to be expected that the desire for choice in education for their children will grow. Their financial capacity to pay for it will almost certainly expand. Government may find it increasingly 'impossible' politically to suppress it. This trend may reverse the 'political impossibility' obstruction to reform.

'POLITICALLY IMPOSSIBLE' TO REFORM EDUCATION? 1979-1989?

To sum up so far:

The rise from 1965 to 1978 in the acceptance of the $\frac{2}{3}$-value voucher from a minority in 1965 to a majority

in 1978, from 30% to 51% in 13 years, is almost $1\frac{1}{2}$%
a year, although more slowly since 1970. There is no
reason to suppose the trend to choice in education
ended in 1978. How it will move in the future, say in
the 10 years to 1989, will depend not least on the trend
of standards in state comprehensive schools, on the
trend in real incomes, the development of higher education, and so on. The trend to choice in education may
accelerate or decelerate. All forecasts are precarious,
though government has to forecast and its forecasts can
be especially damaging since there are no countervailing
competitive forecasts to lessen the damage. Projections
are mechanical extensions of the past, not prophecies.
If the average rate for 1965 to 1978 is projected to 1989,
it will rise from 51% to 67%. If the fall in the rate of
increase from 1965-70 to 1970-78 is continued, it may
continue to rise more slowly. If the 1965-70 rate returns,
it may rise to 78%. The trends are plotted in Chart G.

These percentages would again be higher if measured
as proportions of 'votes' cast.

The voucher could be worth the whole of school
costs, as it was in Alum Rock, is intended in Kent, and
apparently in the trial scheme in Australia, where the
Federal Minister for Education has envisaged parents
taking high school costs of some £750 to £900 to a state
(and possibly non-state) school they prefer.[8] With a
full-cost voucher, the proportion in favour in 1978
would have been much higher than 51%, though not
necessarily 100% for the 'ideological' reason indicated
above (p. 93).

[8] *The Age* (Melbourne), 5 February 1979.

G. **The Suppressed Demand for Choice in Education, 1963 to 1978**
(measured by acceptance of two-thirds value voucher)

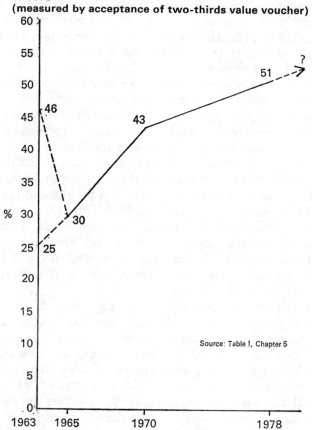

Source: Table I, Chapter 5

B. MEDICAL CARE

Whereas state control of education had developed gradually over a century, state control of medicine was only a dozen years old in the early 1960s. It was easy to obstruct reform of the National Health Service by reinforcing the 'politically impossible' barrier with the plausible defence 'It is still new: give it time'. So we were expected to remain silent as the NHS developed under political and bureaucratic control that was running it with little effort to discover and base it on consumer-priced preference. This defence did not seem to us any more sacrosanct, or any more well-founded in real knowledge of the state of public opinion, than the political refusal to consider reform of state education.

THE HEALTH VOUCHER

As with education, the device of the voucher was used to discover individual ('micro') preferences in medical care, not merely the qualitative generalised wish to have access to services outside the NHS but the quantitative extent to which individuals would *pay* for the option.

Although the education voucher had been persuasively discussed by Professor Milton Friedman since at least 1955,[9] and could be traced back in varying embryonic forms to Francis Cardinal Bourne in 1926[10] and Tom Paine in 1791,[11] we did not know in 1962 of any applications of the device to medical care. It has

[9] *Capitalism and Freedom,* University of Chicago Press, 1962, 'The Role of Government in Education', first published in R. A. Solo (ed.), *Economics and the Public Interest,* Rutgers University Press, 1955.

[10] A. C. F. Beales, in *Education: A Framework for Choice,* IEA, 1967.

[11] He advocated returning £4 of taxes so that poor families could pay school fees: 'Tom Paine's National System', in E. G. West, *Education and the Industrial Revolution,* Batsford, 1975. Tom Paine's argument is in *The Rights of Man,* 1791, republished by J. M. Dent, 1915, revised edn. with a Foreword by Arthur Seldon, 1958.

since come increasingly into the discussion of health policy as a form of earmarked purchasing power to enable people with low incomes and/or high health risk to pay (or insure) for medical care, most recently in 1977 in its most sophisticated form by Professor Alain C. Enthoven of Stanford University, California.[12]

In the IEA surveys the object throughout has been to discover how far people would like the choice between staying with the whole range of services in the NHS and being able to go to medical services available outside it when it suited them and they so wished. It was more difficult to put the private alternative to the state service in medicine than in education. Private schools are a self-contained alternative to state schools: pupils at private schools can return to 'free' state further or higher education (possibly with vouchers for university education after 18, as argued by Professor M. A. Crew and Dr Alistair Young in a Hobart Paper,[13] and by Dr Midwinter,[14] who envisages vouchers for the school years and then extending for periodic spells of education and training throughout life though apparently confined to state institutions). In medicine the NHS supplies public goods (environmental, preventive, etc.), which cannot be bought with the aid of private insurance in

---

[12] 'Consumer-Choice Health Plan' (CCHP), a proposal to Joseph Califano, Secretary for Health, Education and Welfare, Washington, September 1977. (It is summarised in the *New England Journal of Medicine,* March 1978.) Professor Enthoven advocates choice of health financing and organisation methods as the only way to efficiency and consumer satisfaction. He also proposes a voucher to enable people with lower incomes to pay for private health insurance in the market.

[13] *Paying by Degrees,* Hobart Paper 75, 1977.

[14] Address to Yorkshire Region of the Open University, 15 March 1979.

in the market, as well as treatment for long-term, chronic illness which the market may not be able to provide, and family doctors whom people may think they can pay for privately out of pocket without the assistance of insurance. A health voucher would thus cover insurable, personal health services but would leave the individual able to use the NHS as and when he wished.

HEALTH VOUCHERS: SURVEY RESULTS

The first survey in 1963 asked people in the sample not at the time members of private health schemes two questions on the voucher:

> 'Suppose the state was to give a voucher which would cover half/most of the cost of a private room in a hospital, specialist's fees and medicines: would you be interested in such a scheme or not?'

7% were 'very interested' and 20% 'interested', making a total of 27%, in a half-value voucher; 17% were 'very interested', and 21% 'interested', making a total of 38%, in a voucher worth 'most' of the cost of private medicine. The value of this voucher was to indicate a return of public funds contributed (mostly in taxes) to the NHS, but its value was not stated because the cost of hospitalisation could not be obtained from official sources. Nevertheless, replies to other questions indicated that, although the sample was inclined to under-estimate the cost of NHS hospitalisation, they had a better impression of the cost of private hospitalisation.[15] Although the value of the voucher was not stated,

> 'insofar as people broadly knew the cost of private hospitalisation, these figures indicate the degree to which

[15] *Choice in Welfare,* 1963, pp. 20-23.

they would consider choosing a private service and paying the balance'.[16]

In 1965 an attempt was made to make the question more specific. First, we had understood that services covered by private health insurance could be obtained at a cost in premium per head of about £10 per year for a broadly comparable average standard of quality, though with the advantages of choice, etc (p. 105). Secondly, to make the impression of preference or choice clearer, we replaced 'interested' by the more precise term 'accept', though it was not too different to prevent comparison between the two years. Third, we retained 'half' but replaced the imprecise 'most' by the precise 'two-thirds'.

To indicate what private services the voucher (topped up) would pay for, the voucher questions, addressed to the 80% of the sample not members of any form of private insurance, began:

'It is generally agreed that these are the advantages of private health insurance' (a card was shown listing 'able to choose own surgeon, earlier treatment, privacy, more personal treatment').

The two questions continued:

'Suppose that, instead of a National Health Service, the government offered you a voucher worth £5 (£7) a year for each member of your family (including yourself) to help you pay for private health insurance. If you had to add another £5 (£3) for each member, do you think you would accept the offer?'

The £5 voucher was intended to cover half, and the £7 voucher two-thirds, of the cost of insurance. 23%

[16] *Ibid.,* p. 26.

'accepted' the £5 voucher, 30% the £7 voucher. The 23% were thus prepared to top up the voucher by £5 for each member of the family to pay through private insurance for choice of surgeon, earlier treatment, privacy, more personal treatment.

How far the 23% for the half-value voucher in 1965 is directly comparable with the 27% for the half voucher in 1963 depends on how the mild 'interested' (26%) and the stronger 'very interested' (7%) were understood by the sample compared with the more definite 'accept'. Perhaps there was not much change in the two years from 1963 to 1965 in the take-up of the half-value voucher.

Comparison between the 'interest' in the 1963 'most' (of cost) voucher and the 'acceptance' of the 1965 £7 voucher is more difficult. If 'very interested' can be equated more or less with 'acceptance', the 30% response to the £7 voucher in 1965 was stronger than the 17% 'very interested' in the 'most' voucher in 1963, but less than the combined 38% of 'very interested' and 'interested'. To assess whether health vouchers were more or less likely to be taken, topped up and used in 1965 than in 1963, we should have to know how the sample interpreted 'most': £7 is 70% of the cost of £10; 'most' could lie within the range of 51% to 99%. In view of the uncertainties, the line on Chart H linking 1963 and 1965 is shown dotted, and 'interested' and 'very interested' are shown separately as well as together.

The intrinsic interest of these novel investigations was recognised by a scholar in social administration, Dr (now Professor) Gordon Forsyth of the University of Manchester. Despite his general sympathy for the NHS, and the evidence we were discovering of a sizeable

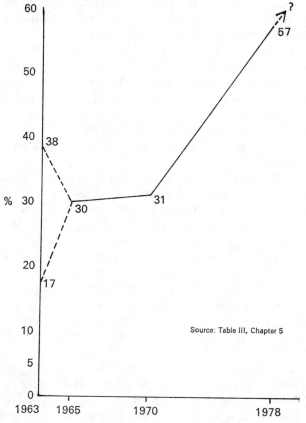

H. The Suppressed Demand for Choice in Medical Care, 1963 to 1978
(measured by acceptance of two-thirds value voucher)

Source: Table III, Chapter 5

dissatisfaction with it which threw doubt on the approval reported by other ('price-less') surveys, he gave a general welcome to the work, although expressing doubt about some results (above, page 90, note 7):

'The economic case for changing the present system of financing the NHS is presented very succinctly in the IEA's *Choice in Welfare 1965* . . . the Institute is right in seeking to test the assumptions governing the present basis of NHS finance . . .'[17]

His doubt was whether the replies to the 1965 voucher questions could 'be regarded as conclusive' because they were 'unclear' in suggesting that the voucher was an alternative offered 'instead of' the NHS. If these questions are taken in isolation out of context of the questionnaire as a whole this may seem so, but read in sequence after the previous questions, and with the explicit introductory references to choice of surgery, earlier treatment, privacy and personal treatment, it is hardly likely that the questions would have been interpreted as offering a voucher in place of the whole range of NHS public (preventive and environmental) services, family doctors, and all the other services associated with it. To the extent that some of the sample may have been misled, the 1965 result should be taken with reserve. In that event the trend can be read from 1970, but the general direction of the trend over the 15-year period seems so clear, despite the changing phrasing of the questions, that the uncertainty about the first two years seems secondary.

In 1970 the voucher questions were preceded by others that made it clear they were not designed to replace the whole of the NHS. Thus an early question asked for opinion on three alternatives—leaving ar-

[17] *Doctors and State Medicine*, Pitman Medical Publishing Co, *op. cit.* Professor Forsyth's criticism, unchanged in the Second Edition, was not updated to the 1970 *Choice in Welfare* results, based on rephrased questions.

rangements unchanged, cash refunds of national insurance contributions, or vouchers 'if the current provision for medical care and attention is not affected'. The question on cash refunds emphasised 'if this does not harm the Health Service' and was followed by the voucher question (addressed to the whole sample; the figures were recalculated to show the replies from those who were not members of private health insurance schemes):

> 'And if the state gave you £7 (£10) a year for each member of the household which could only be spent on health and private health insurance provided you added another £7 (£5) yourself, do you think you would accept this offer or not?'

Compared with the 23% and 30% (of non-members) in 1965, 25% and 29% (of non-members) in 1970 said they would take half-value and ⅔-value vouchers and top them up; there was thus evidently little or no change in the five years. The figures for the whole sample also showed no difference (26% and 31%).

In 1978 the question was unchanged, and again put to the whole sample. The cost of insuring per head had risen from £15 to £60, so the voucher was put at £30 per head at half value and £40 at ⅔-value. This time the change was unmistakable. The 25% for the half-value voucher in 1970 had doubled to 51%, and the 29% for the ⅔-value voucher had almost doubled to 57%.

The 1970 *Choice in Welfare* report remarked that the £15 voucher for insurable personal medical services compared with around £35 for the total cost of the NHS per head, thus leaving funds (£20 per head) to the government for uninsured personal risks and communal (public) health services. In 1978 the £60 cost of insuring per head compared with the NHS total cost of £140 thus leaving £80 per head plus the £20 topping up of the ⅔ voucher, adding up to £100. (In both years the cost of insurable personal services was thus three-sevenths of the total NHS cost.)

The responses in the four years are shown in Table III.

Table III

Suppressed Demand for Choice in Medicine, 1963-1978 measured by acceptance of part-value vouchers

	1963*	1965*	1970	1978
Base	1,599	1,663	2,005	1,992
	%	%	%	%
Would add ½ to ½-value voucher	7†⎫ 20‡⎬ 27	23	26	51
Would add ⅓ to ⅔-value voucher ('most' in 1963)	17†⎫ 21‡⎬ 38	30	31	57

*Excluding those who said they were members of private health insurance schemes.

†'Very interested'.

‡'Interested'.

As with the education voucher, the proportion who would take the ⅔ voucher has risen to over one-half for the first time in 1978. (Rather over 50% would also take even the *half*-value voucher.) And these sharp increases, especially since 1970, in the 'demand' for a choice in medicine, which means the opportunity to pay for an alternative to most of the personal services of the NHS, took place in spite of the doubling in the real cost of the insurance premium per head (allowing for the fall in the value of money).

This steep increase in the proportion of families, hitherto wholly dependent on the NHS, where parents said they would pay for choice, from 30% to 57% in 13 years, a near doubling in frustrated demand, and even more from 31% to 57% since 1970, is nothing short of dramatic. It may not be surprising in view of the increasing publicity given to the deteriorating quality of state medicine, especially since 1970. But it reflects a steady intensification in the coercion of a majority of families whose wish to try private health services, discovered by the micro-economic method of these surveys, is being suppressed by the *political* machinery of majority 'representative' government.*

If the 7% 'don't knows' are excluded, the 57% of the whole sample rises to 62% of 'votes' cast who would take the ⅔ voucher and top it up to pay for personal health services outside the NHS. And if it were raised to the whole cost of insuring for private services, so that the price was reduced, these percentages would also be higher.

SUB-GROUPS

As with the education voucher, women showed as much (but not more) interest in choice as men, and the younger marginally more than the older. But the higher occupational groups were more inclined to accept the cost of adding to both the ½-value and the ⅔-value voucher (Table IV).

Of special interest to social scientists studying the opposing trends of 'proletarianisation' of the middle

---

*'The Potential Market for Medicine with Choice' is outlined in the panel on pp. 110-12, and in Appendix E.

classes and *embourgeoisement* of the rising wage-paid manual workers is the narrow difference between the 55% and 48% of the two occupational groups for the $\frac{1}{2}$-value voucher and between the 61% and 54% for the

---

Table IV

Suppressed Demand for Choice in Medicine, 1978: by Sub-Groups

Questions 20a and 20b

Base: Total sample, 1,992

	Occupational group		Political sympathy		Education	
	ABC1	C2DE	Con.	Lab.	up to 16	over 16
	%	%	%	%	%	%
Would accept $\frac{1}{2}$-value voucher	55	48	61	47	49	57
Would accept $\frac{2}{3}$-value voucher	61	54	67	54	56	63

$\frac{2}{3}$-value voucher. As with education, the rising wage-paid family demonstrated its readiness to dip into its pocket to pay for health care better than the state has claimed to provide equally for all.

Perhaps the high percentage of 30% of the ABC1 group who declined the $\frac{2}{3}$-voucher thought, as with education, that their social connections, cultural advantages, or capacity to make their case with suppliers and officials enabled them to dispense with the sums required out of pocket to supplement the voucher. If so, the conclusion might be drawn that the voucher is even more desirable for the lower-paid occupational groups who lack the skills and influence to compete with the

[Continued on p. 113]

II

THE POTENTIAL MARKET FOR MEDICINE WITH CHOICE

The 57% of the total sample who said in 1978 they would 'top up' a $\frac{2}{3}$-value voucher worth £40 for each member of the family numbered about 12 million aged 18 to 65. Rather over a million are now insured (for themselves and dependants to a total of $2\frac{1}{4}$ million) with the three main insurers, BUPA, PPP and WPA, and eight smaller ones (details, Appendix E). The remaining 11 million could use the voucher to pay for health insurance for themselves and families, a total of, say, 24 million (at $2\frac{1}{4}$ persons covered by each insurer).

● The £40 voucher topped up to £60 (or possibly less) would pay for insurance for a range of private medical services generally including hospital treatment, theatre costs, medicines, etc, nursing at home, consultation with and treatment by specialists (or cash if treated in a NHS hospital).

● Insurance at a higher or lower rate than £60 per head would pay for a wider/narrower range of services on higher/lower rates of reimbursement of fees (below).

● Generally, buyers of the BUPA-type insurance must be in good health and below 60/65; children are generally covered up to 16. People who join before 60/65 can usually continue after 60/65.

● Discounts are usually allowed according to timing of payment (annual or monthly), method (cash, cheque, banker's order, variable direct debit), and kind of membership (as head of a family, member of an association, or employee).

● The fees are reimbursed (partly, largely or wholly) before or after they are paid to the doctor or hospital.

● There is a choice between lower premiums with 'cost-sharing' (the subscriber paying part of each fee, or paying fees after the insurance benefit has been used) or higher premiums for insurance to cover all fees up to a stated annual total.

● State costs and private insurance costs cannot be equated closely because the products differ. The fees for

IIIIIIIIIIIIIIIIIIIIIIIIIIIIIIIIIIIIIIIIIIIIIIIIIIIIIIIIIIIIIIIIIIIIIIIIIIIIIIIIIIIIIIIIIIIIIIIIIIIIIIIIIIIIIIIIIIIIIIIIIIII

II

private services cover elements that may make them better value for money than the (tax-paid) National Health Service:

- *choice of family doctor and specialist (physician or surgeon)*
- *less waiting for consultation, investigation or treatment for 'non-urgent' conditions (gallstones, hernias, arthritis, etc)*
- *choice of timing of consultation or treatment when it suits the patient*
- *choice of place of consultation or treatment where it suits the patient*
- *more personal attention*
- *more privacy if required*
- *more convenience – telephone, etc*
- *more comfort – private TV, bathroom, etc if desired*
- *easier links with family during crises, e.g. flexible visiting, etc*
- *easier links with work during convalescence*
- *consumer authority by direct payment.*

● Eventually insurance costs would be disciplined by competition between insurers, non-profit and commercial.

● NHS services would improve if the shift to private medicine accelerated.

● Insurance costs would be contained, and could be reduced, as new forms of insurance emerged to respond to the new voucher-backed demand for efficient private medical care and with incentives to high-standard service at costs attractive to voucher holders.

● A potentially important source of new insurance cover would be 29 organisations (with 3 million contributors) like the Hospital Saving Association (HSA – Appendix E) which

IIIIIIIIIIIIIIIIIIIIIIIIIIIIIIIIIIIIIIIIIIIIIIIIIIIIIIIIIIIIIIIIIIIIIIIIIIIIIIIIIIIIIIIIIIIIIIIIIIIIII

||||||||||||||||||||||||||||||||||||||||||||||||||||||||||||||||||||||||||||||||||||||||||||||||||||||||

originally (for 2½p or 5p a week) provided 'working-class' families with cash to help in periods of illness. They have been extending their services; HSA's Double 'Crown' Plan, for 50p a week (£26 a year), provides £42 per week (for contributors and dependants) up to 13 weeks a year in hospital, nursing or convalescent home; £28 per week up to 4 weeks a year for recuperation at home; £100 for in-patient chronic mental illness or geriatric treatment; help with NHS charges for spectacles, contact lenses, dental treatment or dentures; a lump sum at child-birth; up to £120 to help pay local authority home-help charges; not least, reimbursement (up to £42 a year) of specialists' fees. Such schemes could increasingly help 'working-class' (and many other) people who want early consultation or treatment, a choice of doctor, and so on, to pay for private hospitalisation or other services. Husbands and wives may join separately, paying together £1 per week or £52 a year, amply covered by the health voucher.

● WPA and others also provide a range of cash payments.

● American Medical International (Europe) offer 'middle- and low-income patients' without other insurance (perhaps because of former ill health) and who have waited long periods for 'non-urgent' treatment (hernias, etc) early attention at three centres; several more are being opened. The fees are paid over 12 months after treatment.

● Hospital Plan Insurance Services provide cash benefits during stays in hospital which can, of course, be used to pay for private fees.

● People are increasingly insuring for dental treatment with Allied Medical Assurance, WPA and elsewhere. Dental surgeons are looking to patients to pay for private treatment.

● More private hospitals are being built to cater for the increasing demand for private treatment (and as 'pay beds' are excluded from NHS hospitals).

||||||||||||||||||||||||||||||||||||||||||||||||||||||||||||||||||||||||||||||||||||||||||||||||||||||||

higher-paid and better connected for their share of state services.

For the reform of health services that may not be delayed for a second 30 years, a fundamental inference must be that the wish of parents to do the best for their family lies near the surface in illness, that rising incomes will enable more wage-paid families to insure for private medical care, and that the more exclusive the NHS is made the more coercive it becomes for more people, not least the wage-earners for whom it was originally and primarily intended.

POLITICAL SYMPATHY

The difference in response between people with opposing political sympathies is also much less than one might expect from the common supposition that the NHS is the shield of the poor. 61% of Conservative and 47% of Labour sympathisers would take the half-value voucher, a wider gap than between the 67% and 54% for the two-thirds voucher. Again the proportion of Conservatives who declined the voucher seems high, and of Labour supporters who would accept it—nearly one in two the lower-valued voucher and more than one in two the higher-valued voucher—much higher than the continued praise of the NHS would suggest.

In all, more than two-thirds of Conservative and over half of Labour sympathisers would evidently prefer a ⅔-voucher, even if they have to top it up, to paying taxes for the NHS. The longer the NHS is maintained, therefore, the more coercion it creates, especially for the people intended to be its main beneficiaries.

EDUCATION OF PARENTS AND MEDICAL CARE
FOR THE FAMILY

A further difference is that between the responses according to education (Table IV). The better (or at least longer) educated responded more favourably than the less well (or at least shorter) educated: 57% to 49% for the ½-value health voucher, 63% to 56% for the ⅔-value voucher. As improving education brings growing demand for more conveniently timed and located medical care, the demand for choice will presumably also grow.

In terms of 'votes cast' all these percentages in favour of the ⅔-value voucher would rise by some 3 to 7 percentage points.

'POLITICALLY IMPOSSIBLE' TO REFORM
THE NHS?

Again, as with the education voucher, there is no reason to suppose the upward trend in the demand for a choice in favour of private medicine through private insurance will have come to a halt in 1978. It will depend not least on the trends in the standards of the NHS and in real income. The trend to choice may accelerate or decelerate. There seems to have been little change between 1965 and 1970. If the average annual rate of increase from 1965 to 1978 of 2% p.a. is projected for 10 years, the 57% of 1978 would become 77% by 1989.

If the health voucher were raised to the whole of the cost of insuring for the range of services supplied by private medicine with the technical skill of the NHS but with the added choice of private medicine, the 57%

of 1978 might have risen sharply, though not as certainly as the trend in the demand for the education voucher, which would offer a complete alternative to the state. As we indicated above, the balance of the average NHS cost (some £80 per head in 1978) after paying for private health insurance would remain with the NHS to cover the services not supplied by private medicine. It would be possible to use the NHS service as required and private medicine when preferred; but, if there were a difficulty in 'returning' to the NHS for some services, some people might not accept the opportunity to pay for private medicine even if the voucher covered its full cost.

The trend and the projection lend little support to Labour politicians who repeat the invocation that the NHS is the envy of the world. Their original understandable euphoria of 1948 is difficult to sustain in 1979. Nor do these findings lend much support to Conservative politicians who might more readily recognise that the NHS was a mistake but who fear that in advocating reform they may leave the public far in the rear. The truth seems to be that the public is a long way ahead of them, in both sexes, in all ages, in all occupational groups, almost as much among Labour as among Conservative supporters, increasingly among the better (longer) educated, and increasingly as taxation is avoided and evaded.

So much for the growing desire for choice in education and medicine. We pass to new evidence that the British are not content with the use by government of the half of their money now taken in taxes.

CHAPTER 6

How Would You Like Your Taxes Spent?

How would the people like their taxes spent?—the *people*,[1] not the politicians, bureaucrats, or other paternalists and pundits.

To our knowledge this question is rarely (if ever) asked in the discussion of 'public' expenditure (a misnomer for expenditure by *government* and its agencies of the *people's* money taken in taxes). But the assumption is invariably that only government can decide how to spend taxes, and the task is supposed to be solely the technical one of devising the required machinery in Whitehall or Westminster. Hence, for example, the brave efforts of Mr Edward du Cann in acquiring more power, staff and expertise for his Public Accounts Committee. Since its main job is to see whether the money granted by Parliament to Departments (Health, etc) has been overspent or misspent, it begs the fundamental questions we are investigating here: whether the money should have been raised in taxes at all and whether it has been distributed according to public preferences.

[1] Verbal style with acknowledgement to Lord Houghton: '. . . the new power [of VAT inspectors] to . . . demand documents and the right to break in . . . is not part of the battle against [tax] evasion as much as part of the counter-attack upon the resentful mood of the people. And I mean the people.' (*The Times*, 16 August, 1976.)

117

DOES GOVERNMENT KNOW?

The usually unstated assumption is that only government knows how and where—on which services and
parts of services—to spend the tax revenue it gathers.
Whether it does or not—a vast debate in the economics
of politics[2]—there is a clear distinction in principle
between the public goods and the private benefits it
provides out of tax (and other) revenue. It has long—
over 200 years since Adam Smith's *The Wealth of
Nations*—been regarded as the necessary function of
government to provide 'public goods' (Ch. 3), for
which a collective organisation such as government is
the only practicable method of supply, and the question
whether government is more or less knowledgeable than
are individuals about their private, personal, family
circumstances, requirements and preferences does not
arise at all. Knowledgeable or not, a collectivity like
government is the only method available to supply
public goods. But in Britain today perhaps two-thirds
of the supplies provided by government are not public
goods. They are predominantly personal services of
which individuals, however fallible, must be assumed
to be better judges than politicians, however benevolent,
or officials, however well-informed they try to make
themselves. It is here that the question must be asked
with which this chapter opened: How would *the people*
like *their* taxes spent on supplying their *personal* require-

---

[2] This is a comparatively recent development in economics which
studies the economics of 'public choice'—the political allocation of resources by government among all activities. It is
discussed by Professor J. M. Buchanan, its senior founding
father, and other economists in *The Economics of Politics*,
Readings 18, IEA, 1978.

ments? Is government now spending it as they would wish?

This is essentially the realm of the two main personal, family services provided by the state—education and medical care—in which the first three IEA field studies investigated personal/family preferences. For since the post-war Welfare State was solidified in 1948, and going back a century to the 1870s, these personal family services have been supplied with little or no effort to discover personal/family preferences.

Individuals elect 'representatives' to Parliament and local Councils who are assumed to know how much they want to spend on each service without asking them. To question this (gratuitous) assumption the fourth survey inquired into how individuals and families themselves would like their taxes spent on personal/family services as well as public goods.

THE LIBERAL-SOCIALIST DEBATE: DIRECT OR INDIRECT 'REPRESENTATION'?

The difficulty that government has in assembling individual/family preferences in order to know how to allocate resources (spend taxes) lay at the root of the fundamental debate between 'liberal' economists, who judged that individual/family preferences could best be assembled through the economic mechanism of the market, and 'socialist' economists, who judged they could best be assembled through the political machinery of elections to representative bodies. After 60 years[3] the

---

[3] The debate was initiated by the 'liberal' economist, the late Professor Ludwig von Mises, in 'Die Wirtschaftsrechnung im sozialistischen Gemeinwesen', *Archiv für Sozialwissenschaften*
[Continued on page 120]

debate has in effect been conceded to the 'liberal' economists; many 'socialist' economists have accepted that markets must be used, as they are in varying forms in the political systems of Yugoslavia, Hungary, Poland and elsewhere. The remaining difference between economists is whether markets require decentralised private ownership of resources, as argued by the 'liberal' economists, or whether it is possible to operate effective markets with state ownership of producing units, as contended by the 'socialist' economists. But there is increasing agreement among socialist economists in the East and liberal economists in the West about the necessity for markets. Politicians in the West have mostly not yet understood that the market is indispensable, though some, influenced in recent years by liberal economists, have seen that it is more efficient than political machinery for supplying personal/family requirements.

Since in Britain the main personal/family services are still supplied by the state, government must be able to claim that it can inform itself of individual/family preferences despite the absence of markets in education, medical care, housing and other personal individual or family services. It claims it can do so by political or 'representative' devices—from national parliamentary and local elections to *ad hoc* voluntary organisations like Parent-Teacher Associations. Politicians in both

[*Continued from page* 119]
und Sozialpolitik ('Economic Calculation in the Socialist Society' in *Journal of the Social Sciences and Social Policy*), 1920, and more fully in *Die Gemeinwirtschaft*, Jena, 1922, translated as *Socialism: An Economic and Sociological Analysis*, Jonathan Cape, 1931.

main parties have also lately evolved parents', patients', and tenants' 'charters' to reflect the people's preferences or interests, at least on paper, a development which we would argue tacitly acknowledges that the 'representative' method of both formal elections and of informal voluntary association has failed.

These devices are innately inadequate compared to markets, fundamentally because they 'represent' consumers indirectly, at second hand, instead of permitting them to represent themselves directly, and because they are exposed to arbitrary differences in power.[4] But some economists have tried to come to the politicians' rescue by devising a concept, the 'social welfare function', which sounds forbidding but is a graphic way of thinking about the task that politicians confront in allocating resources to reflect public preferences. The essence of the idea is that all individual/family preferences can be regarded as averaged and assembled to yield a single ('social') ordering of preferences. (A note on the social welfare function is added at the end of this chapter.)

The question is therefore: Is it possible in the UK to assimilate the preferences of 56 million individuals (43 million adults of 16 and over) or 18 million families or households into one vast 'social welfare function' so that central planning by government can be regarded as based on the preferences of the *people* rather than of politicians and officials? In other words, do the people *agree* sufficiently about how they wish resources to be distributed between all possible uses to make sense

---

[4] 'Representative' machinery is defective because it reflects arbitrary differences in cultural, 'social', political or economic power which are more difficult to correct than differences in income or wealth that decide access in a market.

of the notion of one vast ('social') ordering that will reflect the wishes of everyone?

Since, as far as we know, no-one has tested this massive proposition, we set out in an effort, as a first crude approximation, to discover how similar or how divergent individual/family preferences were in the distribution of tax revenue, first, between seven main forms of government expenditure, including some public goods and some private benefits to represent all government expenditure, and, second, between four main components of the two most personal services supplied by government—education and medical care. They were also asked, for these services and for smaller services supplied by local government, if they were ready to pay higher taxes for services on which they wanted more spent or if they wanted their taxes returned where they wished less spent.

PRELIMINARIES:
ALLOCATION OF A WINDFALL

The study opened with a question to familiarise the sample, as we had done since 1963, with the services we would be discussing and with the notion of making choices in allocating money expenditure between 'public' (government-supplied) services as well as familiar personal/family purchases:

> '. . . imagine that you had been given £2,000 . . . and you have a choice of six ways in which to use it. How would you use it?'

They were shown a card listing three family purchases —'holidays abroad', 'improvements for the home' and 'a car', and three government-supplied services—'education for your children', 'saving against ill-health for treatment and income', and 'saving for retirement'.

To avoid influencing the replies, the six items were rotated at random. The replies are shown in Table I.

The allocations to the three 'welfare' items—education, health and retirement—total 39%. This proportion has fallen markedly since 1963, when it was nearly two-thirds. (The question was omitted in 1965.) The immediate impression is that the people are less concerned about welfare than they were. This conclusion would conflict with most of the remainder of the results, which indicated generally increasing desire for choice in welfare. And the preferences it seems to indicate are unpriced. The lower allocation to welfare may reflect reluctance to supplement the increasing provision of welfare through taxation channelled to the state, where there is no link between tax and service, compared to the direct link between payment and benefit in the markets for home equipment, motoring and holidaying.

DO TAXPAYERS KNOW HOW THEIR TAXES ARE SPENT?

Before asking how taxpayers would like their taxes spent, we tried to discover how far they knew how their taxes were being spent now. The sample was asked to say, or 'guess', how much was spent on each of seven main items of government expenditure out of £100 spent on all seven, together accounting for some two-thirds of the total government spending.

The full degree of knowledge (or ignorance) of the true figures, or even of a very general sense of the orders of magnitude, is indicated by comparing

Table I

Allocation of a Windfall to Welfare and Consumption, 1963-1978

Base: total samples

	1963 (£1,000) Men	1970 (£1,500) Men	1970 (£1,500) Women	1978 (£2,000) Men	1978 (£2,000) Women
	%	%	%	%	%
Welfare					
Saving for retirement	28	25	21	20	15
Education	17	14	19	10	8
Saving against ill-health (treatment and income)	16	15	14	10	13
Combined welfare	61	54	54	40	36
Consumption					
Home improvements	24	27	28	31	34
Car	8	11	8	17	16
Holidays abroad	6	8	10	12	14
Combined consumption	38	46	46	60	64

Note: Percentages do not always add up to 100 due to rounding.

expenditure in 1978 on each of the seven items not with the *average* 'guess' but by the *range* of 'guesses'. (The average 'guess' can conceal the extent of knowledge because it could be somewhere near the 1978 estimate by the accident that the too-high guesses cancelled out the too-low guesses.) The range of guesses is shown in Table II.

The average response initially suggests a tolerably well-informed democracy, except that it (badly) under-estimates government expenditure on retirement pensions and grotesquely over-estimates it on unemployment benefits. It also seems, to a lesser degree, to under-estimate government expenditure on education and over-estimate it on roads. Otherwise it seems to have a reasonably good impression of ranking and orders of magnitude.

This impression of civic literacy is soon weakened, if not destroyed, by studying the dispersion around the averages, which reveal horrendous degrees of ignorance in both sexes, age-groups, socio-economic groups, and political quarters (or halves), although some are more ignorant than others. It should be added that this ignorance is not a criticism of the people but primarily of government, which destroys information by dispensing with the pricing system.

Whatever the state of public knowledge of the true expenditure on government services, public preferences can still differ from government decisions on the allocation of taxes on welfare or consumption, public or private benefits.

Table II

Range of Knowledge/Ignorance of Government Expenditure

Base: total sample 1,992

Question 3

	Latest estimate of expenditure (£ out of £100 on all seven)	Average 'guess'	Range % giving 'guess'				
			£1-10	£11-20	£21-30	£30+	Don't know
	£	£	%	%	%	%	%
Education	24	17	33	40	17	5	5
Retirement pensions	22	11	62	28	4	1	5
Defence	18	16	44	29	17	5	5
Health	17	16	33	44	14	4	5
Housing	15	12	57	32	5	1	5
Roads	2	9	72	20	2	1	5
Unemployment (benefits)	2	20	31	31	20	13	5

Note: The replies were groups of £10; smaller groups would have made clearer the nearness or remoteness of the guesses. 5% were sufficiently certain of their uncertainty to reply 'don't know'. The remaining 95% responded to the invitation to 'guess'.

I. THE MAIN GOVERNMENT EXPENDITURES

(i) INDIVIDUALS AND GOVERNMENT

As a first approximation to the preferences presumed by welfare economists to form the social welfare function, we asked a series of questions to discover if the public thought more should be spent on some 'public' services and less on others. And, to avoid meaningless replies, we built into the questions awareness of the cost of spending more or the tax monies made available by spending less. Those saying they thought more should be spent on one service were promptly asked from where the additional funds should be derived—from other services or from higher taxes. And those who thought less should be spent on individual services were asked to which others they would like the resources moved or whether they wished to have their taxes returned. We thus sought to make the opinions/judgements/decisions realistic by making the respondents aware that they would be making the same real-life decisions on 'spending' their taxes that they made day by day or month by month in spending their earnings ('take-home' pay) left after income taxes were deducted. We thus made each taxpayer-elector-citizen an individual Chancellor of the Exchequer in deciding how he would like 'his' or 'her' taxes spent.

They were then told the estimated 1978 expenditures and asked if they thought more should be spent on any one item, first supposing that the addition came from one or more of the others (and later supposing higher taxes might be forthcoming). That is, they were asked if they would allocate the given tax revenue differently from the way it was being allocated by government.

How much agreement among individuals is required to make government representative?—A simple majority? Two-thirds? Three-quarters? Nine-tenths? Perhaps the required degrees of agreement should differ: less for unavoidable public goods like defence, far more for personal services like health. Even little agreement or a narrow majority would have to suffice for defence, since the alternative might be no defence. But a high agreement would be desirable for health, to justify the state providing health services that individuals could arrange separately and privately to their own requirement.

The first result showed that 70% of the total sample thought more should be spent on one or other of the seven services, at the expense of less spent on the others. This proportion of rather under three-quarters was fairly general in all sub-groups. That is, a large majority would want the existing total expenditure reallocated, and spent differently from the way in which it was being spent by government. Individual welfare functions thus evidently differ widely from the (supposed) social welfare function implied in British government expenditure.

25% said they would want no more spent on any of the seven. 5% did not express their view, or at least said 'don't know'.

(ii) RE-ALLOCATION OF TAX REVENUE ON MAIN NATIONAL EXPENDITURES

How would the 70% like their tax reallocated—on the seven main services we are using to give an impression of public preferences in the expenditure of tax revenue as a whole?

Table III shows the percentages of the total sample

Table III

Public Preferences in the Allocation of Tax Funds, showing Service(s) on which more should be spent and Service(s) from which additions should be taken

Base: people saying more should be spent on one or more: 1,398 (70% of total)

Question 4 at the expense of less on →	Spend more on → Defence	Education	Health	Roads	Housing	Unemployment benefit	Retirement
	177(9%)	246(12%)	675(34%)	415(21%)	179(9%)	80(4%)	158(8%)*
	%	%	%	%	%	%	%
Defence	—	60	56	54	66	52	53
Education	30	—	1	23	12	25	18
Health	12	4	—	5	4	4	3
Roads	8	4	2	—	2	2	6
Housing	42	17	18	2	—	12	21
Unemployment	24	14	13	12	5	—	20
Retirement	25	11	15	11	15	20	—
Don't know	1	2	1	2	1	—	—

*These figures represent the number of respondents and proportion of total sample asking for more to be spent in each category.

Note: Each vertical column adds to more than 100% as many respondents suggested switching tax money from more than one source.

that would like more tax revenue spent on one (or more) of the seven items and from which of the other six services they would wish the revenue to be taken. Thus 34% wished to have more spent on health (the highest proportion) and 4% on unemployment benefits (the smallest proportion). The 34% wanted most of the additional money for health to be taken from defence (60%) and least from education (1%). At the other extreme, the 4% who wanted more money spent on unemployment benefit also wished most to be taken from defence and least from roads. Defence was clearly the main source from which tax revenue was to be switched. On the other hand, 9% wished to spend more on defence; they would take most of the funds from housing, education, unemployment benefit and retirement pensions.

Whether these preferences are regarded as wise or not, long-sighted or short-sighted, they are clearly different from the political priorities imposed by the decisions of government.

(These preferences also reflect the distinction between genuine public goods like defence and psuedo-public goods like education and health. The tendency of respondents to sacrifice defence spending illustrates the necessity for compulsory tax financing where the individual can have a 'free ride'. The benefits of defence spending to each individual are intangible and remote, and he is therefore over-prepared to sacrifice spending on the armed forces for the more obvious direct personal benefits of increased spending on health, education, housing and pensions. That respondents were anxious to increase spending on these services strongly suggests that, as we have argued, they are not public goods. That public goods like defence do not give identifiable, separable benefits explains why individuals would under-spend on them.)

(iii) HOW MUCH MORE?

So far, the answers on *quantity* or *numbers* are crude. It is counting heads without asking the more refined question: '*How much* more?' (or 'How much less?'— below). Yet counting heads is the only question that can be asked by the crude political ballot-box method used to decide the distribution or share of expenditure on government services. This is the 'first-past-the-post' system used in British General Elections. And even refinements, such as various forms of proportional representation, would not indicate the individual judgement of the British on *how much* the government should spend on each government service. In practice, these fundamental political decisions would require opinions on how much *more* or how much *less*, that is, marginal adjustments rather than decisions on totals. These refined individual marginal decisions and preferences can be expressed only in markets, which in Britain work for personal goods and services, because they ask consumers to vote with their money on each commodity or service separately.

So the next question asked: *How much* more should be spent, and from which others should it come?

The results are perhaps the first insight we have— however approximate—into the real preferences of the British people on how they would like their taxes spent. This is the kind of information British governments should have collected—with the vaster resources at their command—if they had wished to check that their policies were based on individual voters' wishes.

The additional amounts that would be spent (shown in Table IV) by those who wanted more spent indicate the degree of dissatisfaction with the government allocation of taxpayers' money.

(iv) PERSONAL WELFARE SERVICES

The 12% who wanted more spent on education (Table III) thought that £1·31 more might be spent out of each £100 spent on all seven items. There was no difference between the sexes.[5] The younger thought more should be added than did the older. The C2DE group thought almost as much should be added as the ABC1. Conservatives wanted a larger addition than Labour. All the results are predictable except the last: it is normally thought that Labour people are keener on education. This finding suggests they realise, as Mr Fletcher says,[6] that it would not be paid for by the wealthy but by the wage-earner in rates and taxes.

Health was voted the largest addition—£3·42—by the 34% who wanted more spent on it, with little difference in the sub-groups except that Labour sympathisers added rather more than Conservative, and women rather more than men. Perhaps the 'Fletcher effect' is at work here too.

The housing addition of the 9% in favour of more expenditure on housing was much less, only £0·87, perhaps because it would go mainly to one in three families, mainly council tenants, no longer thought more deserving than the two-thirds who provide much

[5] The full details are available on computer sheets, which may be obtained from the IEA.

[6] Chapter 1, p. 15.

Table IV

Individual Preferences on Additional Expenditure on Government Services (out of £100 spent on all seven)

Base: all saying more should be spent: 1,398 (70% of total sample)

Question 4b

	Total	Sex		Age		Occupational group		Political sympathy	
		Men	Women	16-34	35+	ABC1	C2DE	Con.	Lab.
	£	£	£	£	£	£	£	£	£
Personal welfare									
Education	1·31	1·30	1·32	1·59	1·11	1·40	1·24	1·54	1·19
Health	3·42	3·27	3·64	3·45	3·39	3·38	3·46	3·19	3·60
Housing	0·87	0·81	0·96	1·20	0·64	0·73	0·97	0·64	0·96
Pensions	0·87	0·69	1·13	0·45	1·18	0·63	1·04	0·81	1·10
Public goods									
Defence	0·87	1·00	0·69	0·69	1·01	1·19	0·66	1·53	0·53
Roads*	2·05	2·25	1·77	1·88	2·19	2·02	2·07	2·35	1·64
Unemployment benefit	0·39	0·45	0·31	0·37	0·40	0·30	0·45	0·22	0·74

*Footnote 7, p. 134.

of their rent subsidies. The sub-group differences were small, except that the younger would add twice as much as the older.

The pensions addition by the 8% in its favour was, relatively to health and even education, niggardly— only £0·87 on average, although women would add more than men, older much more than younger (understandably), the lower incomes more than the higher, and Labour sympathisers rather more than Conservative.

(v) PUBLIC GOODS

So much for the four welfare services. Defence attracted £0·87 on average; predictably, men would add more than women, older more than younger, the ABC1 group much more than the C2DEs, and Conservative sympathisers nearly three times as much as Labour.

The main surprise came in roads,[7] where the average addition from the 21% who would spend more would be no less than £2·05, representing a doubling of the estimated recent expenditure (which the sample had been told before they answered this question). Predictably men would add more than women, Conservative more than Labour sympathisers. But the younger would add rather less than the older. Most surprisingly of all, the lower occupational groups would add as much as the higher, perhaps reflecting the increasing egalitarianism in motoring.

Unemployment benefit was allocated the smallest addition—a mere £0·39. And there was little difference in the sub-groups except that Labour sympathisers would add much more than Conservatives, and the C2DEs more than the ABC1s.

[7] Roads paid for by tolls are not public goods.

II. RE-ALLOCATION OF TAX REVENUE ON MAIN COMPONENTS OF EDUCATION

Before asking for opinions on reductions in tax expenditure, attention was fastened on preferences in the use of tax funds in the two main state services in kind —education[8] and medicine.

(i) KNOWLEDGE OF EDUCATION COSTS

Education was divided into its four main divisions of nursery, primary, secondary and higher.

To test the knowledge of the citizens of a representative democracy of how its taxes are spent on education, the sample was asked to say or 'guess' how much was spent on each sub-division out of £100 of taxes spent on education as a whole. The average of their guesses com-

Table V

Expenditure on the Four Main Kinds of Education: Public Guesses and Recent Estimates

Base: total sample 1,992

Question 5b

	Average 'guesses'	Recent estimates
	£	£
Nursery	14	6
Primary	24	31
Secondary	34	50
Higher	28	13

[8] It has been argued that additional expenditure on higher education can do more harm than good: L. R. Maglen, quoted in M. A. Crew and A. Young, *Paying by Degrees,* Hobart Paper 75, IEA, 1977, p. 18.

pared with estimates of recent expenditures are shown in Table V.

The guesses show extensive lack of knowledge, even as averages, which conceal wide differences and extremes. Only the ranking indicates the correct general impression that most expenditure goes on secondary education and least on nursery education. But the orders of magnitude were mostly far off target.

It seems that citizens of a nation with a century of compulsory education have little general conception of where their taxes are spent. An uninformed populace can hardly choose between alternative policies. What are the 'representatives' in representative democracy supposed to represent?

Whatever the answers to such political/constitutional questions, one defect of a system of state education to set against its presumed advantage is that it destroys information. Few parents of children at 'free' state schools know their annual costs; every parent of children at fee-paid private schools knows their costs as reflected in fees. Parents who know the education costs for their child, because they personally spend their ('take-home') money after tax on it, are more likely to be interested in how their taxes are spent by other people. If the efficient use of scarce resources in alternative uses requires information on costs and values, the tax-paid system is at a massive disadvantage and, by implication, produces massive misdirection as well as massive coercion.

The individual replies indicated even more lack of knowledge (ignorance) than suggested by the average 'guesses': Table VI.

Table VI

Range of 'Guesses' for Expenditure on Education

Base: total sample 1,992

Question 5b	Average 'guess'	% 'guessing'						
		£1–£10	£11–£20	£21–£30	£31–£40	£41–£50	£51+	Don't know / Not stated
	£	%	%	%	%	%	%	%
Nursery	14	50	36	7	2	1	*	4
Primary	24	5	40	43	6	1	*	4
Secondary	34	1	10	36	32	14	2	4
Higher	28	5	24	37	20	8	1	4

*less than 0·5%.

(ii) INDIVIDUAL PREFERENCES IN
TAX-EXPENDITURE ON EDUCATION

Whether individuals in the sample were somewhere near the estimate for 1978 or far away, did they want more or less spent on each sub-division of education? Did they think not enough was spent on nursery infants and too much on university students?—or that more should be spent on primary school children and less on secondary school children?

They were told the estimated expenditures so that they could see how near or far they were. In all (Table

---

Table VII

Public Preferences in Re-allocating Expenditure between the Four main Divisions of State Education

Base: people saying more should be spent: 954 (48% of total sample)

Question 6a Spend more on ➜ at the expense of less on ↓	Nursery	Primary	Secondary	Higher
	517/26%	197/10%	60/3%	319/16%*
	%	%	%	%
Nursery	—	13	43	14
Primary	16	—	20	38
Secondary	70	62	—	64
Higher	23	24	47	—
Don't know	2	3	3	3

*As for Table III, page 129.

Note: Most columns add to more than 100% vertically because some respondents suggested taking money from more than one source. Since some also suggested adding funds to more than one division, the proportion wanting more funds added to the four is less than the sum of the percentages shown against each horizontally* (55%).

VII) 26% thought more should be spent on nursery education, 10% more on primary, only 3% more on secondary, and 16% more on higher education.

In all, including double mentions, 55% wanted resources shifted from some divisions of education to others, including some who wanted shifts to more than one.

(iii) BE YOUR OWN CHANCELLOR:
     RE-ALLOCATING TAX REVENUE

This was the central question: from which other division of education was the addition to come? This is the key decision in all expenditure, public or private: redistributing a given amount of resources between several alternatives to increase the total utility of the whole. In asking where *more* should be spent we were also in effect asking where *less* should be spent. This is where each individual could 'Be Your Own Chancellor'.

The relative proportions who would switch tax funds between the four divisions are paralleled by the relative additions. The largest group of switchers (to nursery education) would on average switch most—£5 (to the estimate for recent expenditure of £6). The smallest group of switchers (to secondary education) would switch least—£0·62 (to the estimate of £50).

The sub-group differences are shown in Table VIII.

(iv) HIGHER TAXES TO ADD TO EDUCATION?

So much for redistributing a given amount of tax funds. The second source of additional money was higher taxes. Question 7 therefore asked:

'Would you personally be prepared to pay more taxes so that more money could be spent in this way [on nursery, primary, secondary or university education]?'

Table VIII

Preferences on Additional Expenditure on each kind of Education

Base: people saying more should be spent on any education: 954 (48% of total sample)

Question 6b

	Average	Sex		Age		Occupational group		Political sympathy	
		Men	Women	16-34	35+	ABC1	C2DE	Con.	Lab.
	£	£	£	£	£	£	£	£	£
Nursery	5·00	4·60	5·51	5·60	4·48	4·50	5·34	4·49	5·39
Primary	1·99	2·21	1·71	1·58	2·30	1·99	1·99	2·22	2·02
Secondary	0·62	0·75	0·47	0·31	0·87	0·35	0·81	0·71	0·69
Higher	3·98	4·45	3·40	3·73	4·19	4·06	3·93	4·25	4·23

The replies were intriguing; we consider they produced a new insight into the preferences that can be discovered when 'cost-conscious' questions impel the respondent to indicate his preferences in the knowledge of the costs instead of answering uncosted questions which mislead him into wanting simultaneously more public services and lower taxes.

Less than one-half, 45%, of those who said more should be spent on one or other of the four divisions said they would themselves pay higher taxes for their favoured increases in expenditures, even after it was made clear that additional expenditure would require more money. 54% replied otherwise: 26% replied outright 'No'; 28% replied 'don't know'. (If this 28% had had more time, and had split half and half between 'yes' and 'no', the 45% 'yes's' would have risen to 59% and the 26% 'no's' to 41%.)

These reactions were spread fairly evenly in the sub-groups. Similar proportions of women as men, of younger as older, and of Labour- as Conservative-inclined said they would pay higher taxes. The better (or longer) educated were marginally less inclined to pay more taxes than the less (shorter) educated. And those who said they would not pay higher taxes were also more or less generalised in all sub-groups, as were the 'don't knows'. It was to be expected that Labour sympathisers would be the more inclined to pay higher taxes for better state education.

Since 48% of the whole sample said more should be spent on one or other of the four stages of education, and 45% of them said they would pay higher taxes to supply the means, only 22% of the whole sample said they would pay higher taxes in order to see more money spent on state education. The remainder would either not want more spent, or would not pay higher taxes, or did not know. Since British government continues to spend more tax revenue on state education it is not, on this evidence, reflecting a majority of public preferences. Whatever else this political decision is based on, it is evidently *not* the public's social welfare function.

The 49% who did not want more spent on any form of education presumably included people who thought the current expenditure was about right and those who thought less should be spent on education. (The sample was not asked directly whether it preferred to see less tax revenue spent on any stage of education, but indicated this opinion by switching tax revenue from them to other stages: Table VII.)

III. PUBLIC PREFERENCES IN TAX-EXPENDITURE ON MEDICINE

A parallel series of questions was asked for medical services.

(i) EXTENT OF KNOWLEDGE

To discover the extent of knowledge (or ignorance) of tax-expenditure on the components of the National Health Service, a question asked the sample to rank the four main components—hospitals, local (family) doctors, prescriptions and public health—in the order in which individuals thought most tax-money was spent. The replies, and the estimated expenditures out of every £100 spent on all four, are shown in Table IX.

As with education, although there is some cognisance of the ranking, hospitals being correctly put first, the

Table IX

**Expenditure on the Four Components of the NHS:
Survey Replies and Estimates of Recent Expenditure**

Base: total sample 1,992

Question 8b	Survey Replies (Averages)	Recent Estimates
	£	£
Hospitals	36	64
Local (family) doctors	21	14
Prescriptions	21	11
Public health	22	11

orders of magnitude are very wide of the mark. Only
£36 out of each £100 spent was attributed to hospitals,
roughly half of the estimate of £64. And the guesses
for the other three were a long way out in the opposite
direction by 'guessing' up to twice the estimates. In the
analysis of the range of guesses, as with education,
only a fraction of the sample came anywhere near the
estimates (Table X).

(ii) PREFERENCES IN EXPENDITURE OF TAX REVENUE: RE-ALLOCATION

As with education, the sample was told the estimate
for the recent government allocation and asked how
individuals would like to spend their taxes. We asked
specifically if they would like more tax revenue spent
on any one of the four NHS components out of a given
total expenditure: Table XI shows the additions as well
as the concomitant subtractions.

Table X

Range of Guesses for Expenditure on NHS

Base: total sample 1,992

Question 8b

	Average 'guess'	% 'guessing'								
		£1-10	£11-20	£21-30	£31-40	£41-50	£51-60	£61-70	£70+	D/k
	£	%	%	%	%	%	%	%	%	%
Hospitals	36	5	14	24	24	20	7	2	1	3
Local (family) doctors	21	17	42	29	5	2	1	*	—	3
Prescriptions	21	24	36	22	9	3	1	*	*	4
Public health	22	23	33	25	10	4	1	—	*	4

*Less than 0·5%.

Table XI

Public Preferences in Re-allocating Expenditure between the Four Main Components of the NHS

Base: People saying more should be spent: 707 (35% of total sample)

Questions 9b, 9c Spend more on ➔ at the expense of less on ↓	Hospitals	Local (family) doctors	Prescriptions	Public health
	265(13%)	248(12%)	45(2%)	254(13%)*
	%	%	%	%
Hospitals	—	30	38	36
Local(family)doctors	24	—	31	26
Prescriptions	48	52	—	42
Public health	26	27	13	—
Don't know	4	2	18	4

*As for Table III, page 129.

Note: Most columns add to more than 100% vertically because some respondents suggested taking money from more than one source. Since some also suggested adding funds to more than one component, the proportion wanting more funds added to all the four is less than the sum of the percentages shown against each horizontally* (40%).

In all 35% wanted more spent on one or other of the four constituents even if it required funds to be taken from the others. The general preference was for a shift from prescriptions to hospitals. Thus 13% wanted more spent on hospitals, of whom about half wanted less on prescriptions. This is a measure of the extent to which tax funds are *not* being allocated in accordance with public wishes, i.e. the nation's individual welfare functions.

61% did not want more spent on one component at the expense of the others. How far this response indicated agreement with the prevailing distribution of tax funds between the four is not known. The 61% would include some who wanted less spent on one or other. To this extent the social welfare function would have misrepresented both the 35% who wanted more spent and the further (unknown) percentage who wanted less spent.

Table XII shows the average additions preferred by the groups favouring additions to each of the four components, and the range and dispersion around the average.

(iii) HIGHER TAXES FOR THE NHS?

So much for public opinion on switching a *given* amount of tax funds between the four components of the NHS. The second fundamental public choice was enlarging the funds applied to the NHS by paying more in taxes. Apart from the small amount of the national insurance contribution that is nominally earmarked for the NHS (some 6%) but of which few of the public are aware, the British Welfare State makes little effort to inform the public of the taxes it pays for the health services it will in its lifetime use as patients.

For 30 years since the NHS was established in 1948 the British have had no opportunity to express through its political machinery either a readiness to pay higher taxes for the NHS or, alternatively, a desire to retain some of its taxes so that it can pay for medical care in other ways. The field study made possible the expression of such an option between these two alternatives.

In view of the widening public distress provoked by increasing revelations of mal-treatment of the two handicapped groups—the aged and the mentally ill—

Table XII

Individual Preferences in Additional Expenditure on the NHS

Base: people who wished to have more spent on NHS: 707 (35% of total sample)

Question 9b

	Average per £100	Sex		Age		Occupational group		Political sympathy	
		Men	Women	16–34	35+	ABC1	C2DE	Con.	Lab.
	£	£	£	£	£	£	£	£	£
Hospitals	3·06	3·41	2·54	2·36	3·59	2·64	3·41	2·93	3·79
Local (family) doctors	2·72	2·61	2·88	2·63	2·77	2·97	2·53	3·02	2·10
Prescriptions	0·34	0·35	0·33	0·28	0·38	0·29	0·38	0·36	0·29
Public health	2·51	2·27	2·86	2·60	2·45	2·53	2·49	2·18	2·60

which it was hoped the NHS would care for better than
would any other system, the restiveness at continuing
queueing for 'cold' (optional, 'elective') surgery, the
diversion of doctors and nurses to administrative tasks,
the growing dissatisfaction and militancy of the pro-
fessionals, the persistence of low pay among the
unskilled employees—all of which it has long been
argued by defenders of the NHS could be put right by
more tax funds—it was to be expected that a very high
percentage of the sample who wanted more spent on
the NHS would pay more in taxes.

The result could not have been anticipated. Only
37% were prepared to pay more in taxes for the NHS,
60% were not. And, since the 37% was derived from
the 35% of the whole sample who thought more should
be spent on one or other of the four NHS components,
the proportion of the total sample who would pay
higher taxes for the NHS is no more than 13%. Presumably 87% would not: they comprised either people who
did not think more should be spent on any component
of the NHS or, if they favoured an addition, who would
not pay higher taxes to provide it; or they did not know.
(Their alternative sources are listed at p. 150.)

The first thought provoked by this response is that
the nation divides almost seven to one (87% to 13%)
against the theory that the troubles of the NHS can be
put right by higher taxes. And the second is that either
many have reached the view that the causes of the
failures lie elsewhere, or that, whatever the effect of
channelling more money into the NHS, they would
prefer to use it themselves on other goods or services.

Even more noteworthy is the uniformity of the view
in both sexes and the age, occupational, and political

Table XIII

Opinion on Readiness to Pay more in Taxes for the NHS

Base: people who wished to have more spent on NHS: 707 (35% of total sample)

Question 10

	Total	Sex		Age			Occupational group		Political sympathy	
		Men	Women	16-34	35+		ABC1	C2DE	Con.	Lab.
	%	%	%	%	%		%	%	%	%
Yes	37	36	40	35	39		37	38	35	44
No	60	61	57	61	58		59	60	62	52
Don't know	3	3	4	3	3		4	3	3	4

sympathy groups (Table XIII). No more C2DE than ABC1 people would pay more in taxes to be spent on the NHS. More Labour than Conservative sympathisers were prepared to pay more in tax for what Labour claims is its most characteristic achievement in compassionate social engineering. Yet the distribution of preferences between support for and opposition to higher taxes for the NHS suggests far from universal readiness among Labour sympathisers to make sacrifices to support it. 44% of Labour sympathisers who wanted more spent on one or other component of the NHS said they would pay higher taxes, 52% said they would not. Since only 35% of all Labour sympathisers said they would like more spent on one or other component of the NHS, the percentage of all Labour sympathisers who would pay higher taxes is no more than 16%. The remaining 84%, apart from a very small percentage of 'don't knows', either did not wish to see any more spent on any part of the NHS or would not pay higher taxes to provide the addition.

(iv) OTHER SOURCES OF FUNDS

Where else would money for medicine be obtained? These sources would be of two kinds: taxes channelled to government and charges (prices) paid direct to doctors, for prescriptions and to hospitals. The next question asked the whole sample whether the government could derive more money from other sources (by implication for the NHS). 56% replied it could, 40% that it could not. The 56% named the other sources: lotteries 29%, social security 14%, civil service 10%, cutting out waste 6%, overseas and defence 4%, road tax 3%, gambling/betting tax 2%.

(v) MORE MONEY FROM CHARGES?

Before asking opinion on the second source—direct charges, or higher charges—we tried to discover the extent of knowledge of the current cost of the three personal service components of the NHS (we treated the fourth, 'public health', as a public good for which charges were not feasible or economic). The average replies are shown in Table XIV. The next question then began by stating the most recent estimated expenditure before asking whether respondents thought more should be paid; the estimates are also shown for comparison.

Table XIV
Expenditure on Health Services: Estimates and Guesses
Base: total sample 1,992

Question 12a

Service	Unit Costs	Average Guess	Recent Estimate
		£	£
Family doctors	per visit	6·50	4·00
Prescriptions	per prescription	1·51	1·50
Hospitals	weekly	101·30	250·00

The calculated estimates were intended to be for a visit to a family doctor, for a single prescription, and for the cost of a week in hospital. The intention was to discover how far individuals were prepared to pay more for health care by paying direct charges or higher charges.

The average guess for family doctor visits was £6·50 against the estimated cost of £4, which is higher than many doctors charge for a single visit. Whether by chance or judgement, many individual guesses were near this figure. 52% guessed £2 to £5, 23% £6 to £10, 14% over £10, 7% £1 or less. But since it does not pay family doctors (at least directly in fees), the public could not be expected to know this figure.

The estimate for each prescription was calculated at £1·50. (The most up-to-date is around £2.) The average guess came out about right, which seems creditable since individuals know only the nominal charges they have paid for each prescription (20p since 1969), whatever the cost. But the individual guesses were distributed oddly around two most common guesses: 33% guessed over £2 and 26% guessed 51p to £1. The guesses between £1 and £2 were, surprisingly, less common: 16% thought between £1·51 and £2, 8% between £1·01 and £1·50. 12% guessed far too low at 50p or less.

If the public has any idea at all about health costs, it might have been supposed to be able to make a creditable guess at hospital costs. The weekly cost was chosen as the figure that might be in the minds of respondents when considering whether they were prepared to pay a (new) charge towards it. The estimate of £250 was more applicable to the lower-cost provincial hospitals: London (especially teaching) hospital weekly costs were higher, usually much higher. The figure was intended to cover 'hospitalisation' itself, excluding fees for surgery or other special treatment. But just as they had under-estimated the proportion of total NHS costs spent on hospitals (36% against the estimate of 64%), so the sample severely under-estimated hospital costs. Against the estimate of £250 their *average* guess was barely over £100 (£101·3). The most dedicated supporters of the Welfare State can hardly suppose such widespread and extensive misapprehension to be politically healthy.

The range of guesses, moreover, was very wide. Of the total sample, comprising 1,992 people of both sexes, from 16 to 65 in all socio-occupational groups and 75 towns, boroughs, suburbs and villages of England, Scotland and Wales, nearly ⅔ (63%) guessed £100 *or less*. Only 6% guessed over £250.

Even if, as many observers think, it is immoral to charge hospital patients (though the moralists do not distinguish between charging before, during, or a long time after the hospital stay or allow for spreading the cost before and after by insurance), it may be desirable at least to inform people of the cost after they have recovered. If it is immoral to pay, it can hardly be immoral to know. It may be potentially even more immoral not to know, since not to know may encourage the natural tendency of both doctor and patient to over-caution and to prolong hospital stays at the expense of patients on waiting lists and of the community in general which has to pay in taxes for prolonged hospitalisation.[9]

The degree of lack of knowledge, and of severe *under*-estimation, was generally uniform in all sub-groups, with some differences in the most incorrect lowest guesses. In the £50 or less group (27%) there were apparently more women than men, many more in the lower than in the higher occupational groups, and more Labour than Conservative sympathisers. If we combine the £201 to £250 and the £251 to £300 as being

[9] Economists have referred to the self-interested tendency as 'moral hazard', since the patient does not bear the cost of prolonging hospitalisation. To the extent that the private patient has his charges covered by insurance, moral hazard can be lessened by cost-sharing of various kinds—co-insurance, deductibles, etc.

the more or less correct range, it was guessed by only 7%
of the total sample: men were better than women, the
upper occupational group was better than the lower,
and Conservative sympathisers better than Labour, but
not by much. (Computer sheets available.)

(vi) MORE MONEY FOR HEALTH CARE?

Whatever the state of their knowledge or ignorance of
hospital, doctor or prescription costs, the whole sample
was told the latest estimated costs and asked:

'Are there any [of the three] you think it would be a good
idea if people were asked to pay more towards than they
do now?'

This question (and several others) was the outcome
of much deliberation between us and our research
advisers. The intention was to ask whether there was a
readiness to pay charges (or higher charges) as the
alternative to the first method (asked earlier) of paying
more in taxes. To have done so clearly the question
should have been micro-economic:

'Would *you* pay more in direct charges rather than in
taxes?'

It is not clear that all respondents understood the
question in this sense. 44% thought 'people [should be]
asked to pay more', 55% did not. Men and women did
not differ, neither did the younger and the older. More
of the ABC1s than of the C2DEs thought people should
pay more, and more Conservative than Labour sympathisers.

Question 12b also asked those who replied 'Yes' to
say 'how much more they ought to pay'. The replies—
presumably indicating the charges (or additional

charges) it was thought people should pay—are shown in Table XV, with wide ranges round the average.

Table XV
Additional 'Payment' (Charges) for Health Care
Base: those who said people should pay more for health: 871
(44% of total sample)
Question 12b

Service	Average
	£
Doctor (per visit)	2·90
Prescription (each)	0·57
Hospital (per week)	36·80

The full sample was then asked:

'And are there any which you think it would be better if you could pay less towards—if necessary having to find your own way of meeting the costs?'

This phrasing was intended to ask whether people thought they ('you') should pay less *in taxes* and then pay privately by charges and/or health insurance reimbursement, and may have been clearer in the interview than it seems in isolation. The replies, significant or not, were: 73% 'none', 9% doctor, 11% prescription, 11% hospital.

Opinion on paying more taxes for better state welfare or lower taxes and paying privately is indicated in the more general questions (both micro and macro) and their replies discussed in Chapters 3 and 5.

IV. PUBLIC PREFERENCES IN
TAX EXPENDITURE ON
LOCAL AUTHORITY SERVICES

Local government spends about 10% of gross domestic product in Britain, and the central government contributes about 60% of the cost from national taxes. Are counties, boroughs and other local governments spending the people's rates and taxes as *they* would prefer? (In the economist's language, whatever the accuracy or inaccuracy of the national welfare function, how representative or unrepresentative are local authorities and their municipal welfare functions?)

As before, the interest was in discovering whether and how the people would like the existing rates and taxes redistributed between local government services; if they wanted more spent on one or other local service, whether they would like less spent on others or would pay higher rates; and if they would like less spent on one whether they would like more spent on the others or have their rates returned for them to pay for private service in charges, fees, etc.

Since the purpose was to obtain general indications rather than detailed prescriptions, the opening question listed four services in which there was general interest or recent debate—libraries, school meals, sports facilities, and police, the average amount spent on them per adult a year by local authorities as a whole, and asked the sample, first, whether any of the four should have *less* (tax) money spent on it and to name them. Here again, it did not matter whether the estimated expenditures were precise or up-to-date; whatever the expenditures, the object was to obtain general reactions

on how far the use of tax money was broadly approved
or not. The results are shown in Table XVI.

The reaction to the opening question—whether
people thought less should be spent—was intriguing,
perhaps because, to our knowledge, it has never before
been asked in social studies. Almost everyone had an
opinion (only *one person* said 'don't know'.) Two-thirds
(65%) thought expenditure should not be reduced on
any of the four, but 35% thought it should: 18% on
libraries, 12% on school meals, 4% on sports, and 4%
(surprisingly) on police. (Some thought less should be
spent on more than one of the four.)

The two-thirds were almost uniformly spread in
both sexes, age-groups, occupational groups and, more
surprisingly, political sympathies.

On the other hand, there were some differences
between the sub-groups in the views on which of the
four services should have less spent on them. Perhaps
surprisingly, since libraries were originally intended to
give the common people access to improving books, the
lower occupational groups were more (22%) in favour
of reduction in state expenditure on them than were
the higher groups (14%), and, even more unpredictably,
so were Labour sympathisers (23%) than Conservative
(16%). There was little difference between men and
women or between younger and older people. The question suggests itself: who uses public libraries? Are they,
like other government services, making for more rather
than less unequal distribution? And, if so, why do politicians persistently claim that 'public services' are the
great contribution that government has made to improve
social conditions and ameliorate social inequality?

Differences in the sub-groups on school meals were

Table XVI

Public Preferences in Re-allocation of Rates and Taxes in Local Government

Base: total sample 1,992

Question 13a Percentage wishing less spent on:	Total	Sex		Age		Occupational group		Political sympathy	
		Men	Women	16-34	35+	ABC1	C2DE	Con.	Lab.
	%	%	%	%	%	%	%	%	%
Libraries	18	20	17	16	20	14	22	16	23
School meals	12	13	12	10	14	19	8	17	8
Sports	4	4	4	2	5	4	4	5	3
Police	4	4	3	6	2	3	4	2	4
None	65	63	68	69	63	65	65	66	66

more predictable. Rather more of the older than the younger wanted less spent on them, many more of the higher than the lower occupational groups, and also many more Conservative than Labour sympathisers.

The small 'vote' (4%) for cuts in sports-on-the-rates and police were spread more or less in all sub-groups.

WHAT TO DO WITH THE 'SAVING'?

The consequential and more searching question was on whether the saving in the rates on one or other of the four services should be used to increase expenditure on one of the others or to reduce the rates. This must be the first and only opportunity a representative cross-section of British ratepayers has had to answer this key question, which no political party has asked nor has created machinery for asking. If 'informed' observers were invited to say what replies they expected, they would have little convincing grounds for their judgements. The results are shown in Table XVII.

The 35% of the total sample who thought *less* should be spent on one or more of the four local services divided in proportions few would expect. Two-thirds (62%) thought the saving should be applied to other local services. One-third (34%) wanted it returned in rates. As proportions of the total sample, therefore, some 21% wanted rate revenue redistributed between the local services and 12% wanted the reduced expenditure returned in rates.

Redistribution was preferred fairly evenly in all sub-groups, except that the younger were predictably more in favour than the older. Conversely, more of the older than the younger favoured a return of rates. More

Table XVII

Public Preferences in Re-allocation or Reduction in Rates/Taxes as a Result of Lower Expenditure

Base: people saying local authorities should spend less: 689 (35% of total sample)

Question 13b

Preference	Total	Men	Women	Age 16-34	Age 35+	Occupational group ABC1	C2DE	Political sympathy Con.	Lab.
	%	%	%	%	%	%	%	%	%
Reduction	34	33	36	30	37	29	38	35	31
Re-allocation	62	62	61	67	58	65	60	61	65
Other answers	2	3	2	1	1	4	1	2	3
Don't know	2	2	3	3	2	4	1	3	2

intriguingly, so did many more of the lower occupational group than the higher. And again there was no large difference between Labour sympathisers, who might have been expected to be much more in favour of redistribution than lower rates, than Conservative sympathisers, who might have been expected to prefer lower rates to redistribution.

When the whole sample was asked if they thought local authorities should spend *more* on one or other of the four services, 26% were not in favour, but 6% wanted more on libraries, 14% on school meals, a surprising 33% on sports, and the largest proportion, 37%, wanted more spent on the police: Table XVIII.

The 26% opposed to more expenditure on any of the four services showed some interesting differences in the sub-groups: more women than men, rather more older than younger, somewhat more Conservative than Labour sympathisers, but surprisingly no difference between the two occupational groups.

Libraries attracted more support from men than from women, and from the upper than the lower occupational groups. But there was no difference between the political groups. Perhaps the middle occupational group Labour sympathisers use public libraries more than lower occupational group Conservatives.

School meals predictably attracted more support from the lower occupational group and Labour sympathisers.

Sports were supported more by the younger than by the older. There was no difference between the two occupational groups but a higher vote among Labour than Conservative sympathisers. As noted previously,

Table XVIII

Public Preferences in Re-allocation of Rates and Taxes on Local Government Services

Base: total sample: 1,992

Question 13c

Percentage wishing more spent on:	Total	Sex		Age		Occupational group		Political sympathy	
		Men	Women	16-34	35+	ABC1	C2DE	Con.	Lab.
	%	%	%	%	%	%	%	%	%
Libraries	6	8	3	6	5	9	4	5	5
School meals	14	14	13	16	13	9	17	11	17
Sports	33	34	31	39	28	32	33	29	36
Police	37	40	33	34	39	40	35	42	37
None	26	23	30	23	28	27	26	27	23

the social division is not co-terminus with the political.

The (perhaps expected) difference in support for more expenditure on the police did not emerge. Men were surprisingly rather more in favour than women.

Finally, those who wanted more rates spent on one or more of the four local services were asked whether the addition should come from redistributing existing rate revenue or from higher rates. Only 21% thought rates should be raised. The remainder wanted less spent elsewhere: Table XIX.

Regrettably the length of the questionnaire precluded further questions on the individual services from which the additional expenditure should be transferred.

* * *

So much for the first, if only approximate or crude, attempt to discover how the British people would like their taxes spent, including rates, and therefore to measure how far government is interpreting its wishes. The conclusion must be that rates and taxes are not being spent as most people, if truly reflected in the sample, wish. And to this extent British government cannot claim to be representative. The social welfare function implicitly operated by government is not the amalgam of 21 million individual welfare functions.

Nor does there seem to be a 'consensus' on the way in which current government expenditures should be re-allocated to satisfy the preferences of some citizens without simultaneously frustrating the preferences of many or most other citizens. Whatever the differences in the interpretation of some of the findings, the full range of preferences revealed by these surveys confirms the central argument (outlined in Chapter 4 and else-

Table XIX

Public Preferences in Re-allocation of or Increase in Rates/Taxes as a Result of Higher Expenditure

Base: people saying local authorities should spend more: 1,473 (74% of total sample)

Question 13d

	Total	Sex		Age		Occupational group		Political sympathy	
		Men	Women	16-34	35+	ABC1	C2DE	Con.	Lab.
	%	%	%	%	%	%	%	%	%
Re-allocation (less elsewhere)	71	69	73	73	69	70	71	71	67
Higher rates/taxes	21	22	19	18	22	20	21	21	26
Other answers	6	7	4	5	6	6	6	7	6
Don't know	4	4	5	5	4	5	4	4	3

where) that the more of the people's money is spent by politicians the less representative of their wishes 'representative government' becomes. And the converse is that the less representative it becomes in supplying personal services the more coercive it has to be, the more conflict it creates, and the more it threatens social harmony.[10]

This conclusion is not unexpected, especially by economists who have been studying government 'failure' as well as market 'failure' in the efficient distribution of scarce resources. Government has no machinery for measuring individual preferences in the expenditure of taxes on public goods proper like defence. That explains why it cannot represent private preferences or public opinion on the services it must provide willy-nilly because they cannot be provided in the market. But it strengthens the view that, if government does not or cannot represent the people, it should relinquish the state or municipal supply of essentially personal goods and services and allow the people to represent themselves directly, and therefore more effectively, in education, health and welfare generally by using their money in the market.

Majority rule is therefore not only coercive but also inefficient.[11] The more widely it is used the more defective and deceptive it proves to be. Representative democracy has become a misnomer for the over-ruling of individual choice.

[10] 'Change by Degree or by Convulsion', in *The Coming Confrontation,* IEA, 1978.

[11] Professor William Mitchell, *The Anatomy of Public Failure,* International Institute for Economic Research, California, 1978.

A Note on
the Social Welfare Function

Individuals are assumed to be able to 'order' differing bundles of 'goods' when confronted with the task of choosing between them, to express either preference or indifference. They are presumed to be able to construct such an ordering for all possible alternative bundles. They are considered rational if their choices satisfy certain widely accepted characteristics such as consistency, economy, choice. The modern theory of consumer choice is based on these fundamental propositions.

In practice, not all choices are made by individuals. In part because of 'market failure' arising from the presence of public goods,[1] externalities,[2] or natural monopolies,[3] in part because of the 'meddlesome' behaviour of government that thinks it can improve on markets,[4] many choices are made collectively. The problem then is: what rules should govern the making of collective choices that can be in some sense derived

[1] Goods which must be purchased collectively: defence, Chapter 3.

[2] Damaging effects on third parties who are not compensated by the user, e.g. atmospheric pollution.

[3] Industries where direct competition would be impossible or 'wasteful' because very large units have very low costs.

[4] 'Meddlesome' government is discussed by Professor C. K· Rowley in *The Economics of Politics,* Readings 18, IEA, 1978·

from the differing preferences of individual citizens? One approach to this problem, following Professor Kenneth Arrow of Harvard University, is to try to construct a 'social welfare function',[5] which will translate or map private preferences into public policies to satisfy a minimum of the desired characteristics. In a sense, this represents a search for a 'collective choice' counterpart to the theory of individual choice.

Arrow's search for a 'desirable' social welfare function or 'constitutional rule' has failed. His 'impossibility theorem', indeed, established that, in societies where individuals differed in their preferences, there were no conceivable constitutional rules that would always satisfy his 'desired characteristics' when individuals were faced with conceivable alternative choices. This failure has not deterred hosts of economists from continuing the search for a collective paradise and others from more modest attempts to see how much 'desired characteristics' must be sacrificed before the constitutional rules become effective.

Unfortunately for the economists who were hopeful of this approach, the social welfare function literature contains two false assumptions which have serious implications for the role of the state: first, that a small élite would have full knowledge of all individual preferences over all social alternatives; second, that it would follow impartially any constitutional rule (e.g. a simple majority) selected as a basis for arranging (or mapping) individual preferences into social policies.

These two false assumptions have led some economists to propose an exaggerated role for government.

[5] The Arrow error is discussed by Professor James M. Buchanan in *The Economics of Politics*.

Only recently have economists, led by the 'public choice' school in the USA, focussed on the economics of politics (or 'public choice')[6] and demonstrated the dangers of such unrealistic analysis of the political process. For many years Professor F. A. Hayek had contested the 'constructivist' basis of these assumptions.[7] Where reliable information has been collected relating to evaluation by individuals of the *costs* as well as of the *benefits* of competing social policies, some mapping might be attempted, for example by employing constitutional rules such as majority votes. It is this approach, carefully circumscribed to reflect its limitations, that has been adopted by the Institute in this study of public preferences.

[6] The economics of politics or public choice is explained by Professors Buchanan, Rowley and others in *The Economics of Politics.*

[7] His latest analysis is in *Law, Legislation and Liberty,* 3 volumes, Routledge & Kegan Paul, 1973 to 1979.

CHAPTER 7

Tax-Benefit: Profit or Loss?

Long before our first survey in 1963 it was clear to independent analysts that the post-war promises of party men to guarantee the best standards in education and medical care for all without charge would arouse expectations that could never be fulfilled by tax-financed monopoly. By 1979 it should begin to dawn on the most casual observer of Britain's intensifying economic and social tensions that a major cause lies in the progressive expansion of governmental spending on welfare.

THE LOGIC OF FAILURE

So long as resources are scarce there will be a tug-of-war between alternative ways of using them to satisfy diverse preferences which cannot all be met in full. In competitive markets this unavoidable source of disharmony is resolved by higgling over price with the minimum of social conflict.[1] Where consumers enjoy maximum freedom to allocate their limited income between the widest conceivable variety of food, clothing, domestic equipment, motoring, books, leisure facilities and so on, they are guided—and ultimately disciplined —by the price mechanism. In the real world we soon discover we cannot have all we would like. In our every-

[1] The full argument will be found in *The Coming Confrontation* (especially in the Prologue by Arthur Seldon), Hobart Paperback 12, IEA, 1978.

day lives we come to terms with the ineluctable human condition of going without or postponing many desirable purchases.

When politicians set out to extend 'free' (or heavily-subsidised) services to all-comers they destroy (or disrupt) this balancing mechanism between supply and demand. Offered the illusion of 'something for nothing', voters naturally press for more and better education, improved health services, cheap housing, subsidised transport, social benefits and whatever else is going. But when confronted with the hidden cost in rising taxes, the supposed beneficiaries behave perfectly logically in trying to resist footing the bill. It is naïve for politicians to ask people to behave 'reasonably' by curbing their demands for better services, or, alternatively, by accepting the need for still higher taxes. Adam Smith understood better 200 years ago when he singled out the most potent drive of human conduct as 'the uniform, constant and uninterrupted effort of every man to better his condition . . .'. It is in full accord with this prime mover that everyone should press the government to provide more of those services they value whilst insisting that the cost should be met as far as possible from taxes falling on others.

It is, therefore, not the people but the politicians who lack logic and reason. By divorcing payment from choice in 'free' services, they have converted rational voters into chronic schizophrenics. In the political market there is no way for the individual to vote for those improvements in welfare services for which we have seen (Chapter 5) he would be willing in the economic market to sacrifice alternative forms of consumption, i.e. to pay from his own income.

It is no wonder that the claims on 'the state' since the war have escalated even faster than the mounting taxes to finance them. Here is the main cause of the growing burden of the government (so-called 'public') sector at the expense of marketable output,[2] the piling-up of inflationary pressure, and the resulting resort to such short-term, constrictive, divisive, delusive, inexpedient expedients as prices and incomes policy. All stem from the pretence that scarce resources can be given away without costly consequences. The deepening economic crisis is basically and unavoidably the predictable result of supposing that the declaration of 'good intentions' (reinforced by political opportunism[3]) was a sufficient substitute for rigorous economic analysis which demonstrated that government could not wish away the necessity to make agonising choices between desirable objects.

All governments have to impose (unwelcome) taxes to pay for public services that cannot be provided through the competitive market. But even for national defence and (most) police services, everyone likes to be a 'free rider' in the sense of enjoying the government's protection while escaping the taxes necessary to pay for them. That is another reason why, if citizens are expected to pay their taxes willingly, politicians should keep services financed by compulsory levies to a minimum. It is the failure of successive governments to understand this limitation that accounts for growing concern about the extent of tax avoidance and evasion.

[2] R. Bacon and W. Eltis, *Britain's Economic Problem: Too Few Producers,* Macmillan, 1976.

[3] Gordon Tullock, *The Vote Motive*, Hobart Paperback 9, IEA, 1976 (2nd impression, 1978).

At the same time, as politicians have extended the range of 'public services', the increasing evidence of their incompetence has begun to raise deeper doubts about the democratic process itself.[4]

CLAIMS ON NATIONAL RESOURCES

The present scale of government expenditure is not the result of a systematic review of the relative merits of the alternative public (monopoly) and private (competitive) methods for achieving the best use of scarce resources in the light of preferences and possibilities in the 1970s. It is largely the outcome of a patchwork process since before the beginning of the century whereby new social and economic commitments have been assumed by politicians in response to short-term pressures, often under the influence of passing fads and fashions. It has been thought sufficient for the advocate of each new social programme to make a case 'on its merits', which has often meant on its effectiveness in winning the good opinion of a handful of leader-writers or the votes of an organised minority interest-group. There is no attempt to weigh the effect of adding another straw to the camel's back or to measure the long-term consequences of fanning the flames of taxpayer resentment and resistance.

The present state of the political game in government spending is summarised in Tables I to III which show the claims on national resources of the main components of central and local government expenditure in 1977.[5]

[4] Professor F. A. Hayek's essay, 'Will the Democratic Ideal Prevail?', in *The Coming Confrontation, op. cit.*

[5] 1977 is the latest year for which these figures were available at the time of writing from the *National Income and Expenditure* Blue Book.

Table I
**Central and Local Government Expenditure on
'Public' Services: 1977**

	£ million
Military defence	6,850
Foreign service	400
Police, prisons, fire service	1,725
Parliament and law courts	375
Roads, street lighting	1,510
Public health, land drainage, coast protection	285
Water, sewage, refuse	560
Finance, tax collection	805
TOTAL	12,500

Source: *National Income and Expenditure,* 1967-77, HMSO, 1978.

Table I brings together all the heads of spending on what are generally, but often mistakenly,[6] regarded as 'public' services, that is, services appropriate for collective provision financed from tax revenue. The total cost of these services in 1977 amounted to £12,500 million, equivalent to 20 per cent of total government spending (shown in Table IV as £62,500 million) or 10 per cent of national income (shown in Table IV as £125,000 million). Table II shows the more debatable forms of government spending mostly falling outside the strict category of public goods that have to be supplied collectively. It includes subsidies paid (mostly) to the suppliers of goods and services who in many cases could finance themselves through the market from increased charges—all the more easily if the suppliers and their

[6] Some 'public services' (refuse collection, water, some roads, police and fire services, and more) could be provided in return for direct payment by customers, as argued and documented by Arthur Seldon in *Charge*, Temple Smith, 1977.

Table II
Government Subsidies: 1977

		£ million
Overseas aid		920
Transport, communications		1,000
Employment services		890
Industry, trade, research		1,425
Agriculture		1,000
Parks, libraries, museums, arts		780
Local government and other services		1,300
	TOTAL	7,315

customers were relieved of the high taxes levied to finance these subsidies.

But even if we allowed that all these 'public services' and subsidies were justified on some interpretation of 'the public interest', their total cost accounts for less than one-third of all government spending. The striking fact revealed by Tables III and IV is how far welfare expenditure has come to dominate the combined budget of central and local government.

Table III shows the growth of spending in the four main categories of welfare (education, health, housing and social security) from a total of £5,100 million in 1963 to £34,600 million in 1977. Because the comparison of monetary totals over this period is rendered largely meaningless by the accelerating debasement of money through the inflation of prices, Table IV relates welfare growth to national income since 1963 in a number of ways. In the first place, it shows that the cost of welfare has increased from below 44 per cent of total government spending in 1963 to 56 per cent in 1977. Since

Table III
Government Spending on Welfare: 1963, 1965, 1970 and 1977

	1963 £m.	1965 £m.	1970 £m.	1977 £m.
Education	1,400	1,700	2,800	8,300
NHS	1,100	1,400	2,300	8,000
Housing	600	950	1,250	5,100
Social Security	2,000	2,400	3,900	13,200
TOTAL	5,100	6,450	10,300	34,600

government spending has itself risen as a proportion of national income over this period, the Table also shows that welfare spending has risen still more sharply—from 18 per cent to 27·5 per cent—as a proportion of national income. Finally, to remove as far as possible the distorting effects of inflation, the Table includes an index of the rise in general prices from which is calculated the increase at constant prices (or in real terms) of government spending and national income. The lower half of Table IV enables us to see that, between 1963 and 1977, the period of our four surveys of public preferences, there was a rise in real national income of the order of 30 per cent while total government spending rose by over 50 per cent and spending on welfare roughly doubled.

If we take the national income as reflecting the scarce resources available to the community each year, we can say that during a period of 14 years in which real resources increased by less than one-third, governments by arbitrary decision unrelated to real public preferences increased their spending by more than half. Of

Table IV

Government Spending and National Income: 1963, 1965, 1970, 1977

	1963	1965	1970	1977
at current prices	£m.	£m.	£m.	£m.
Total Government Spending	£11,650	£14,150	£21,850	£62,500
Spending on Welfare	£5,100	£6,450	£10,300	£34,600
Net National Income	£28,250	£33,100	£47,200	£125,000
	%	%	%	%
Welfare as Proportion of Total Government Spending	43·5	45·5	47	56
Welfare as Proportion of National Income	18	19·5	22	27·5
Total Government Spending as Proportion of National Income	41	42·5	46	49·5
	Index: 1963=100			
Index of Consumer Prices	100	108	137	342
Index of National Income (at constant prices)	100	108	122	129
Index of Total Government Spending (at constant prices)	100	115	136	155
Index of Welfare Spending (at constant prices)	100	117	147	198

Source: *National Income and Expenditure* Blue Books, HMSO. National income is measured at market prices, net of capital consumption.

this increased government 'take', the lion's share (60 per cent) was accounted for by spending on welfare. The increasing diversion of slowly growing resources to rapidly rising government (and especially welfare) spending is graphically illustrated in Chart I (p. 178).

WHO GAINS FROM WELFARE?

Even so large a share of government spending (56 per cent) or of national income (27·5 per cent) might be thought worth devoting to social welfare if there was reason to believe that the majority, or even a sizeable minority, of the population would otherwise be denied access to schools, hospitals, doctors, homes or pensions through lack of income. Such a justification cannot survive exposure to the evidence assembled from official statistics in Table V. It is clearly impossible to summarise the financial circumstances of families of all conceivable sizes, composition and incomes. But from the extensive data published by the Central Statistical Office (CSO), Table V sets out the balance-sheet of taxes paid and social benefits received by the average of all families studied in two categories: two non-retired adults, and two adults with from one to four children.[7]

Since averages conceal the circumstances of untypical families, it would be impermissible to draw large conclusions from close statistical comparisons. Yet the

[7] Based upon regular 'Family Expenditure Surveys', the benefits allocated to families account for 47 per cent of total government spending, but 82 per cent of all spending on welfare (excluding mainly administration of social security, personal social services and capital investment in housing and social services). The taxes paid by families cover 62 per cent of government revenue (excluding company taxes, unallocated indirect taxes and borrowing).

I. Growth in National Income and Government Spending, 1963-1977

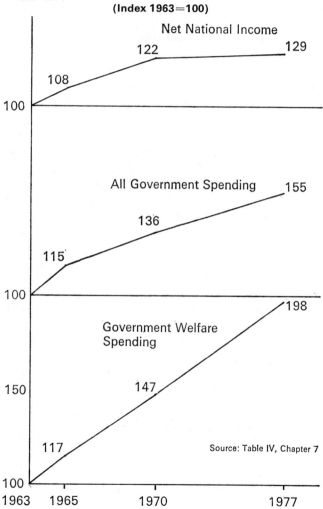

(Index 1963=100)

Net National Income

122   129

108

100

All Government Spending   155

136

115

100

198

Government Welfare
Spending

150   147

117   Source: Table IV, Chapter 7

100
1963   1965   1970   1977

picture revealed by the CSO analysis provides vivid proof that the present scale of governmental welfare cannot be justified on the ground that its recipients would otherwise be sunk in poverty. When tax costs are brought into the reckoning, we might almost say that the Welfare State impoverishes even the poorer of its intended beneficiaries. If we start from the *average* family of two non-retired adults, we find from Table V/A that they receive much less in welfare benefits (£599) than they pay in taxes (£1,938), so that their original average family income of £5,037 is reduced by 27 per cent to a 'final income' (net cash plus benefits) of £3,701.

Since this average irons out large differences between the 1,611 two-adult families in the sample, the CSO divides them into 10 equal groups (deciles) each composed of 161 families with average incomes ranging from below £1,868 for the lowest decile to over £8,230 for the highest. If we ignore the lowest decile of families who derive more than half their incomes from social benefits, we can examine the balance between benefits and taxes for the second and third poorest deciles. From Table V/A it will be seen that the families in the second decile on average receive benefits of £1,021 and pay taxes of £903, thereby gaining £119 on their original income of £2,375, an addition of less than 6 per cent.

From the third decile upwards, we begin to encounter the mass (80 per cent) of families who are net losers from the tax-welfare merry-go-round. Thus the 161 families in the third poorest decile gain on average £611 in benefits but lose £1,187 in taxes, ending up £576 worse off with net incomes reduced by 18 per cent to £2,584. It is hardly necessary to consider the figures for

Table V

Tax-Benefit Balance-Sheet in 1977

A. Households of 2 non-retired adults

(Based on a sample of 1,611 households)

	Average		2nd decile	3rd decile
Original Income		£5,037	£2,375	£3,162
ADD BENEFITS				
Cash	324		697	306
Education	47		57	70
NHS	228		267	235
		+ 599	+1,021	+ 611
LESS TAXES				
Direct	1,153		383	636
Indirect (net)	785		520	551
		− 1,938	− 903	− 1,187
NET GAIN/LOSS		− 1,339	+ 119	− 576
Final Income		£3,701	£2,494	£2,584

the higher deciles since from the fourth upwards the net loss begins to move from 20 per cent to well above the 27 per cent which we found for the average of all the 1,611 families in this group.

It may be supposed that the picture would be very different for families with up to four children, since they naturally draw more on education, family allowances and other welfare benefits. Table V/B shows that the picture is surprisingly similar: the *average* family (with an income of £5,083) finishes up with a loss of £626 (12 per cent). The second decile shows an average net gain

TAX-BENEFIT : PROFIT OR LOSS ?   181

Table V

Tax-Benefit Balance-Sheet in 1977

B. Households of 2 adults and 1-4 children

(Based on a sample of 1,924 households)

	Average		*2nd decile*		*3rd decile*	
Original Income	**£5,083**		**£2,923**		**£3,551**	
ADD BENEFITS						
Cash	283		321		190	
Education	507		481		413	
NHS	326		338		332	
Welfare Foods	55		54		41	
		+ 1,171		+ 1,194		+ 976
LESS TAXES						
Direct	994		328		597	
Indirect (net)	803		559		682	
		− 1,797		− 887		− 1,279
NET GAIN/LOSS		− 626		+ 307		− 303
Final Income	**£4,457**		**£3,230**		**£3,248**	

Source: 'The effects of taxes and benefits on household income, 1977', in *Economic Trends,* HMSO, January 1979.

of £307 (10·5 per cent) and the third a net loss of £303 (8·5 per cent), which almost exactly cancel out if we combine the two groups. In other words, the average of the second and third deciles shows a starting income of approximately £3,240, from which £1,083 of taxes is deducted and £1,085 of benefits is added, leaving a net gain on the tax-benefit profit and loss account of almost precisely nil (exactly £2 if the figures are read literally).

The break-even point between benefits and taxation

is related to average family (more exactly 'household') income. Average full-time earnings of all adults in 1977 were £3,500 a year (£70 a week). Furthermore, if we omit families composed of retired pensioners, the majority of households included two or more workers, although the incomes of wives, children and part-time workers would generally be well below the average of £3,500 a year. The unmistakable lesson to be distilled from the CSO analysis is that most families more than pay their own way in taxes for all the benefits they derive from the Welfare State, and that the excess of taxation begins to be imposed at incomes well below the average earnings of a single adult worker.

It may be asked: Are these circular comings (of benefits) and goings (of taxes) worth all the effort, expense, bureaucratic ballast, disincentive to effort, tax avoidance and evasion, tension between tax-payers and tax-gatherers, aggrandisement of government, monopolisation of personal services, suppression of innovation, strengthening of trade union hegemony, debilitation of the family, loss of talent by emigration?

An even more fundamental question is: Does this vast structure of swings and roundabouts reflect or respect real public preferences? Our inquiries indicate they do not. Then what can be done? And what (or who) stands in the way? To these questions we now turn.

CHAPTER 8

Choice for Public Policy

We have argued that the provision of so-called 'free' welfare services denies citizens the freedom of choice they enjoy as consumers in the competitive market. The statistics now confirm that even families with incomes well below the average pay dearly for what might more accurately be described as their politically-administered ration of welfare. Politicians (and trade union leaders[1]) compete in claiming compassion for the poor. Until recently, at least, they found it politically profitable to pose as public benefactors, acting like a child's conception of a benevolent Santa Claus. It was this sham that led Dr Colin Clark to ask what we would think of a Father Christmas

> '. . . who came round on Boxing Day to collect the entire cost of the gifts he had handed out, together with a substantial commission for himself for having organised the distribution'.[2]

Mounting opposition to higher taxation—which would have risen further if Chancellors since 1973 had

---

[1] Partisan and unrepresentative trade union leaders have masked their pursuit of narrow sectional interest by urging government to increase the 'social wage' of state benefits—for which their members were then called upon to foot the bill in higher taxes.

[2] Colin Clark, *Poverty before Politics,* Hobart Paper 73, IEA, 1977, p. 11.

not improvidently financed 10 to 20% of spending from borrowing—has compelled even a Labour Government to restrain the growth in government expenditure. The result is intensifying and generalised public discontent. Parents and patients (especially on waiting lists) are dissatisfied with standards in schools and hospitals; workers employed in them complain about low incomes; and more public commentators are beginning to acknowledge the excessive costs of the burgeoning bureaucracies, partly because more of them are experiencing its consequences in their private lives as tax- and rate-payers, husbands, wives and parents.

EQUALITY VERSUS PROGRESS

If politicians, officials and academics who proclaim their compassion were truly concerned with the poor, they have a wide choice of more effective policies to ensure that none falls below a civilised minimum standard of income and social welfare. So long as backward-looking defenders of the Welfare State obstruct reform, they are not only denying the poor minority more generous, selective support. They are also preventing the affluent and middle-income majority from devoting a larger slice of their rising incomes to more and better welfare services of their choice. Nor can such condescending paternalists—in all parties—take refuge behind the sociological slogans of 'equality' versus 'double standards'. However emotionally satisfying it may be, the claim of equal treatment in schooling or medical care is daily falsified by the advantages enjoyed by articulate people with political pull or social push. As the evidence of such abuses multiplies, the self-advertised idealists turn sour in pursuing a vendetta against the small rump of private welfare where parents sacrifice other consumption to pay for choice in schooling or medical care.

The egalitarians in welfare have succeeded only in checking the diffusion of higher standards which in motoring, television, kitchen equipment and holidays have—within a single generation—brought the 'privileges' of a minority successively within reach of widening majorities. That is the way of a dynamic, competitive market economy in which producers are always seeking to extend their sales by offering improved products as cheaply as latest techniques make possible. And this truly progressive mechanism is frustrated in services run by government monopoly which complacently asserts that none shall enjoy advantages that cannot immediately be extended to everyone.

FIRST—A MINIMUM STANDARD

In education and health, the false—because unrealised and unrealisable—claim of *equal* standards for all stands in 1979 as the main barrier to *better* standards for all, though in varying measure. Once freed from subservience to political slogans, there is no lack of alternative welfare policies from which to choose. Appendix F lists more than 50 IEA studies which have pioneered and helped keep alive thinking about ways in which varying degrees of market arrangements can improve on British pensions, housing, education (primary, secondary and higher), medical care and local government services.

The first requirement for progress in social policy is that lip-service to equality be supplanted by an effective universal minimum standard. Since the essential precondition of acceptable standards in food, shelter, warmth and the rest is adequacy of income, the government's duty is not to supply goods or services for everyone, but to direct financial support to the minority with inadequate incomes. State education and the NHS are *supply* responses to a deficiency of *demand*. The method increasingly favoured by independent students of social policy is a reverse income tax which assesses family need for subsidy by the same pervasive process which the Inland Revenue applies in assessing ability to pay income tax. A number of IEA studies have recommended such a reform,[3] the latest and most comprehensive being published in 1977 under the challenging title *Poverty before Politics*.[4] This report summarised the findings of an extensive research project undertaken by Dr Colin Clark, the distinguished but unacknowledged pioneer of national income statistics as well as a seminal thinker on social policy. In place of the Topsy-like growth of British post-war social security financed by mis-named national 'insurance' contributions and general taxes, Dr Clark proposed moving in stages towards a single system of topping-up incomes below a specified minimum and reducing taxes for others who would thereby be enabled to insure themselves and their families against unemployment, sickness and retirement, and ultimately to pay for services in kind.

From elaborate calculations on government statistics of taxation, incomes and expenditure, he concluded that

---

[3] *Policy for Poverty,* Research Monograph 20, 1970, reported the findings of an IEA study group in favour of a minimum income guarantee based on a reverse (or negative) income tax.

[4] Hobart Paper 73, *op. cit.*

a reverse income tax would halve the annual cost of social security (then running around £12,000 million) and enable high taxes on incomes to be cut drastically from a range at that time of 35% to 98% to the narrower, lower range of 20% to 50%. Not least among the advantages of this reform would be to end the absurdity of paying families with children higher (untaxed) unemployment benefits than the net value of (taxed) earnings from employment.[5]

SECOND—CHARGE FOR NON-PUBLIC SERVICES

The historic justification for governments to provide 'free' services was that the poor could not pay for them. Rising incomes yielded by the market economy—in the face of mounting political obstruction—have progressively reduced the number of families to which this incapacity might apply. The introduction of a reverse income tax would finally put an end to this argument for government provision beyond the defined range of public goods that have to be settled through the ballot-box.

If the present generation of politicians persists in heeding the coterie of unrepresentative activists rather than the aspirations of ordinary people revealed in these surveys, if they shrink from the confrontation with obstructors of competition and choice, if, in short, they fail to allow individuals to escape from nationalised and politicised welfare, it is likely that half-hearted measures will provoke more bitter antagonism between the people and the party men who over-rule them. There is no longer any excuse for delaying fundamental reforms. Faced with the negative choice between

[5] Ralph Howell, *Why Work?*, CPC, 1976.

deteriorating services or higher taxes, the only positive
alternative is to make a start with charging for the
personal and family services government now (in-
adequately) finances through (excessive) taxation. We
have seen that most families are already paying indirectly for all the welfare services they consume. What
possible objection can there be to bringing this payment
into the open by direct charging for schooling, hospitals,
GPs and the rest? Reduced taxes would enable most to
pay or to insure for payment. Topping-up low incomes
would enable the poorest to meet the cost of all services
that cease to be supplied 'free'.

The advantages would be many and mutually reinforcing. Income from charges would reduce the amounts
governments now have to find in taxes to finance 'free'
services. Lower taxation would enable more families to
pay (or insure) for private welfare services in the market.
At the same time, charging would lower the present
barrier of 'double payment', thereby encouraging more
private schools, health insurance schemes, even universities[6] and hospitals, to develop by offering wider
variety in methods of payment and services. Individuals
who pay charges towards the cost of public services are
less likely to put up with the patronising, paternalistic,
insensitive attitude of public 'servants' who now pass
themselves off as public benefactors. Competition from
a stronger private sector would further compel government services to be more responsive to their customers
or risk losing them at an accelerating rate.

If charges for most state welfare services were set as

---

[6] The University College at Buckingham has since 1976 demonstrated some of the boons—for students and staff—that only
private enterprise can pioneer.

a start at one-third of the full cost, the initial savings in government spending would be of the order of £5,000 million even after allowing a generous margin for the additional subsidies to poorer families through the reverse income tax. A fuller review of the advantages of introducing pricing to a wide range of mis-named 'public services' will be found in *Charge*[7] where Arthur Seldon concludes that only about one-third of all government expenditure on benefits in kind is on collective services that have to be financed by taxation.[8]

THIRD—MAXIMUM CHOICE

In principle, the reverse tax could gradually be extended to replace ultimately all or most 'free' education, medical care and other benefits in kind that government now supplies to all and finances from high taxes on the supposed beneficiaries. At this stage in the argument, proposals for reform are likely to provoke protests from paternalists whom Dr Clark accused of basing policy on 'a massive contempt for the poor'. The familiar argument is that if government reduced taxes and topped-up low incomes sufficiently to enable everyone to pay for their chosen welfare service, some (many? most?) would spend the cash on frivolous consumption. This accusation rests on a distinction (from 19th-century social inquiry) between 'primary' poverty (=inadequate income) and 'secondary' poverty (=mis-spending of an adequate income, mainly through ignorance of value for money). It is a revealing com-

[7] Temple Smith, 1977.

[8] These issues are also extensively discussed in *Pricing or Taxing?*, Hobart Paper 71, 1976, which includes our oral evidence to the Layfield Committee on local government finance.

mentary on a hundred years of compulsory state education that parents are judged to remain so incapable or
uncaring that they would neglect spending on family
welfare, despite, moreover, cash subsidies or reduced
taxation.

In any event, our results reveal that, despite decades
of suppression of family decision, people with lower
incomes soon evince interest in choice (as the few extracts
in the Introduction (pp. xxii-xxiii) graphically drama-
tise) once it is available. Not least, we refer again to the
evidence unearthed by Professor E. G. West[9] that,
many years before the Welfare State and long before
the beginnings of state education in 1870, some poor
families were sending their children to school (*without*
compulsory school attendance laws) and paying fees.

It now appears that the very extension of dependence on government for welfare has robbed many
potential private customers of the experience and judgement they have acquired in the market for goods and
services on which they are well used to spending their
own money. So it may be a justified concession to the
paternalistic approach to base the next stage of policy
for welfare on the imposition by government of minimum standards in education and medical care, provided
they are not pushed too high and so used to keep out
newcomers to protect members of the National Union
of Teachers or the British Medical Association, or other
defensive interests.

Even the most exacting concern for minimum standards, however, does not require government to maintain its present near-monopoly in the supply and

---

[9] *Education and the State,* IEA, 1965, 2nd edn., 1970; *Education
and the Industrial Revolution,* Batsford, 1975.

finance of schools, universities, teachers, hospitals, doctors, nurses and all that goes with them. No more is required than for government to stipulate minimum standards, enforce them on suppliers by inspection, and ensure all families have sufficient money—or the wherewithal—to pay. Reverse taxes could enfranchise even the poorest with the cash to spend in the freer democracy of competitive markets on approved education and personal health services[10]—as on food, clothing and other equally basic necessaries. But to guard against the fear that some would spend money on other things, the device of the earmarked voucher was conceived as a way of supplying the purchasing power whilst avoiding the temptation for recipients to indulge other lines of consumption.

VARIATIONS IN VOUCHERS FOR EDUCATION

The voucher is a highly adaptable device capable of meeting differing policy and administrative requirements. To begin with, the value of an education voucher might be fixed for everyone at the full cost charged by an efficient school that conforms to the stipulated standard. It might be confined to state schools, although if benefits of competition and choice are to be fully reaped, it should be equally exchangeable for private education. If combined with reverse taxes, the voucher could vary in value according to income and family circumstances. Even if the voucher value is the same for all parents (or

[10] Congenital or mental infirmities unsuited to insurance would call for public provision or subsidies—but not all 'catastrophic' illness, which in the USA can be covered by a modest premium, just as householders are familiar with insurance against the comparable catastrophe of their homes being destroyed by fire.

varied only with the age of their children), it could be included in the parents' tax assessment as a benefit in kind or earmarked cash and taxed according to the PAYE code number. Any such variations of the voucher could either be imposed on everyone (or on all above a specified income), or be available as an option to parents wishing to contract out of state education.

So long as private schools at least measure up to the prescribed standard, there is no case in equity for excluding them from the scope of the voucher. It remains true that parents already paying for a private education out of savings or taxed income could be said to gain an uncovenanted bonus from the offer of a voucher, although the effect would simply be to relieve them of paying twice. That may, however, be a reason for setting the voucher value at a proportion of the total cost. Another reason is that the larger the number of parents who took up the voucher, the larger the demand for changes in schools to cater for such parental and pupil preferences. There would almost certainly be a demand for more emphasis on structured teaching, probably for religious and single-sex schools, and at the same time possibly for more uninhibited 'free-learning' methods. Competitive markets combine standardisation in some products and services with wide diversity in others. The same mixture would now be more visible in schooling if politicians, urged on by administrators and faddists, had not increasingly tried to steam-roller policy into a single mould.

After a century of centralisation, choice in education should be expected to usher in large though gradual changes. An optional voucher that started at, say, half or two-thirds of the cost of standard schooling would have the twin advantages of switching demand away from unpopular state schools gradually and also of reducing the total cost of state provision plus vouchers that would continue to fall on tax revenue.[11] A further gain in the longer run would flow from the effect of competition and cost-consciousness in reducing the waste in state schools where costs are now often higher than in comparable fee-paying private schools.

ALTERNATIVES FOR HEALTH

Although the voucher could be applied as an alternative to universal state health services, there might be advantages of discovery through diversity in social experimentation by starting with the different solution of allowing individuals to contract out. It will be recalled from Chapter 3 that over half the sample in the 1978 survey preferred this option (C) to either the present policy or the concentration of state provision on people in need (Ch. 3, Tables I and IV, pp. 45 and 50).

All that would be necessary is for the government to credit the cost of hospital, consultant and GP services on the tax assessment of individuals who can show they are covered by an approved private medical insurance policy that provides equivalent services. The effect on total government spending would depend on where the balance was struck. Thus the Exchequer would sacrifice some revenue (in addition to the credits given to the 5 % already insured privately), but it would of course save

[11] The literature on vouchers is increasing rapidly both from academic and political sources. Kent County Council published in 1978 its report on a pilot scheme and there is recent information of an experiment in Australia. Initiatives on education credits in British Columbia and Washington are approaches to education vouchers.

expenditure on government health services no longer required by people switching to private doctors, specialists, hospitals and other facilities. So long as people contracting out are credited on their tax (or reverse income tax) returns with a sum less than the average cost of the services they forego, there must be a net saving of revenue available to reduce taxes.

The main objection to permitting contracting out by tax reduction, rather than offering a voucher, is that the advantage of choice would not be available to families who pay little or no taxation. Yet our survey showed that the majority of C2DEs (52%) was not far below that of ABC1s (58%) in favouring freedom to contract out (Ch. 3, Table III, p. 49). Furthermore, the larger the savings in government spending from reform of welfare policy, the further taxes could be reduced and the more people would pay little or no tax—thereby losing the tax advantage from contracting out of state health services.

This frustration of choice for people with lower incomes, who may still wish to pay something towards private medical care but could not meet the full cost, could be met in two ways. For those in paid employment a refund of 'tax' could be financed from the compulsory 'National Insurance' contribution paid by them and their employers. Since this now amounts to a 20% levy on all wages above £17·50 per week,[12] it would provide an ample inducement even for low-paid workers who wished to exercise the choice of private health insurance.

Yet another source of customers for contracting out

[12] Raised to £19·50 per week from 6 April, 1979.

would be the growing number of companies, large and small, that would pay the health insurance premium for their staff (and increasingly for their work-force) as a valued fringe benefit for the employee and a guarantee of better or more prompt treatment (including periodic medical check-ups) that would yield some return to the employer in reduced absence through sickness and lengthening delays in surgery.

PRIVATE MEANS BETTER MEANS MORE

It may be questioned whether private education or medical care will necessarily be 'better' than the state service. The answer is that it must be regarded as better by people who choose to pay for it, or else they would save their money and settle for the 'free' service. This reply prompts the further question whether parents are the best judges of schools or prospective patients of doctors and hospitals. The answer is that so long as there are minimum (though not restrictive) standards in schools, hospitals, teachers, and doctors (which is more than appear today in some state establishments), the customer cannot choose a lower standard and is entitled to his subjective judgement on what is better. Parents could take advice, as they do now before making many purchases; but it would be they who finally decide in the light of their own judgement instead of bureaucrats in the light of bureaucratic convenience.

So we are left with the conclusion that unless private education and medical services are better—in respects valued by their customers—they will not develop further but will dwindle. So long as they are better—at least in the judgement of more families than now use them

—private schools, hospitals and GPs will attract paying customers and additional spending into welfare.

The final doubt that conscientious sceptics raise is whether the resulting expansion of private welfare must be at the expense of the state service. This appealing but unfounded anxiety is based on the fallacy we encountered earlier that the supply and demand of particular resources is so 'inelastic' that they do not adapt themselves to changes in price and other circumstances. If more people are prepared to spend a larger slice of rising incomes on better (private) schools and hospitals, it follows that the total resources drawn into these services will be increased at the expense of more spending on other goods and services on which the money would otherwise have been spent. It is government control that has restricted the number of doctors and tightening restrictions over NHS and private practice that have driven many doctors to emigrate and made British hospitals increasingly dependent on immigrant doctors.

THE URGENCY OF REFORM

The latest, more acute, spasm of renewed economy, threatened stringency and endemic discontent, that by early 1979 have crowned many decades of intensifying political control of education and health services, underlines the urgency of radical reform in welfare.

Our surveys leave no doubt. The majority want more freedom of choice. Given choice, they would spend more on welfare. If they spend more, government would be able to spend less. If government spends less, it can reduce taxation. And if taxation can be reduced sufficiently, many other freedoms will be extended. Not least, we can enjoy more choice between ways of spending the increased wealth that would follow the combination of less taxes, more freedom and competitive markets—which could work their magic in education and health services as in other aspects of our individual and family welfare.

For democrats the puzzling question remains: Why has public policy continued so long to over-rule choice in welfare? Experience in other countries confirms our analysis that alternatives are technically practicable. The dramatic growth in public support for choice revealed in the four surveys since 1963 shows that reform is no longer—if it ever was—politically impossible. The remaining barrier is the resistance of politicians, demagogues, bureaucrats and their trade unions to changes that would disturb their already failing collective grip on the apparatus of state welfare.

REPRESENTATIVE GOVERNMENT OR REFERENDA

Even if the evidence in our four field studies and the argument we and IEA authors generally have developed are accepted by a new government, it may hesitate to implement reforms that are desirable, that are administratively practicable, and that the people show they prefer because it fears possibly fierce social tension with the interests that will resist them.

This is not a criticism of the people who may feel tempted to offer strong resistance to avoid disturbance to their lives. Choice in welfare will have to be introduced more rapidly, and will require redeployment more extensive, than can be accommodated by the staffing policies of governments anxious to avoid friction with civil service or local government unions by keeping jobs going until retirement.

Unless such a reforming government came to power with a large majority, its authority may need to be strengthened or 'legitimised' by a stronger and more incontrovertible indication of public support. A more direct mandate from the people in referenda may therefore be thought desirable to introduce the reforms without disturbing social peace.

Happily it is easier to use the technique of referenda in 1979 and beyond than it was until recently. The June 1976 referendum on entry into the Common Market and the March 1979 referenda on devolution have familiarised the British people with direct voting on specific issues, though it has long been familiar, in one form or another, to the Swiss, the Americans, the Scandinavians, the Australians, the French and the Irish. There are weighty arguments against referenda. In our view they may now be outweighed by two advantages. First, it is the only way in which individuals can indicate they wish personal services to be shifted from government to the market, where individual choice can prevail. Second, as we have argued, a referendum may be essential for government to introduce the reforms to prevail over well-organised sectional interests without violent confrontation.

THE FINAL ENEMY

So the final enemy turns out to be nothing more than a variant of the familiar resistance of entrenched producer-interests to the disciplines of an open competitive society that would make them serve the long-run interests of consumers.[13] For all the rhetoric about good intentions in 'the public interest', it is self-regarding sectional interests which—however unconsciously—prevent the abandonment of policies that have not, will not, and cannot achieve their declared purposes.

Can we take hope from the Keynesian dictum that all vested interests are in the end vulnerable to 'the gradual encroachment of ideas'? It is not difficult to show that ideas on welfare have changed—and even that the long-run interests of politicians, civil servants and union members would be better served by deferring to the desire for choice of their voters and paymasters. The interests that have battened upon and buttressed state education and medical care must therefore find it increasingly impossible to preserve the façade of serving the public.

For how much longer can the party men boast of the achievements of the Welfare State, or the swollen bureaucracy take pride in presiding over a further decline in standards? The mounting confrontation in 1979 *via* strikes, threats of strikes and fears of strikes should help to teach the unions that when the only employer is a state monopoly, lax discipline, weak management and over-manning are no recompense for low wages.

The failure of the half-century experiment in state control over welfare is now making it politically profitable for new policies that will win support by returning to the sovereign people their freedom to spend their own money on education, medicine and other services

[13] The general argument is set out more fully in *Not from Benevolence* . . ., Hobart Paperback 10, and *Can Workers Manage?*, Hobart Paper 77, IEA, 1977.

of their choice. If those who have ruled the roost with such deplorable results are so short-sighted as to think they can retain their control over the lives of the people, they will eventually have to learn better—perhaps through escalating and still more bitter confrontations and even convulsion.[14]

---

[14] The possibilities and dangers for social peace are indicated in *The Coming Confrontation*, Hobart Paperback 12, IEA, 1978, which provided a timely curtain-raiser to the intensifying dissensions which marked the opening of 1979.

Epilogue

When full allowance is made for possible differences in construing the detailed findings of our four field surveys since 1963, one central conclusion emerges. It is no longer possible to doubt that the representative samples of varying ages, sex, social, occupational and educational background and apparently contrasting political sympathy reflect a growing preference—shared by a clear majority in 1978—for changes in policy that would enable families to choose education and health services outside the state.

It is hardly a new discovery that all political leaders have lost touch with the voters they claim to represent. A striking example was the massive rejection in the March 1979 referendum by Labour voters in Wales of Labour's devolution Bill. More generally, recent years have seen a decline in popular support for the ruling party until in 1974 Mr Wilson's Government was sustained by no more than 29% of the total electorate. It risks making a mockery of democracy for governments resting on such narrow support to claim its authority for extending coercive powers over the spending of half the national income created by the efforts and enterprise of all the people, including the 71 per cent.

When we reflect that at least a quarter of state spending is on schools and health services which increasingly fail to reflect the wishes of 70% or more of the (Labour) party supporters commonly thought most sympathetic to state control, the risk to democratic allegiance is seen to be not hypothetical and prospective but present and pressing.

The best that might be said for politicians is that they mean well. But when they persist in policies that have failed on the pretext that they are more 'compassionate', they invite the rejoinder that they are simply trying to do good at other people's expense, indeed at the expense of the supposed beneficiaries. Numerous IEA studies and other works by economists and social scientists in Britain and North America have demonstrated that there are better ways to welfare than the centralised, tax-financed monopoly services supplied by the state and its multiplying agencies over which the conscripted consumers have no control. Politicians naturally prefer state services as a means of making voters dependent on the political process.

It is thus a common refrain of politicians that reducing taxes must produce deterioration in public services. For example:

> 'The crude choice is often put to me,' said the then Chief Secretary to the Treasury, Mr Joel Barnett, on 6 February, 1979, 'simply in the phrase "cut public expenditure". It all sounds so easy. But what this crude choice means in practice is diminishing the social and environmental provision we are entitled to expect as citizens of a civilised country (and in which we want to make further improvements—smaller classes, shorter hospital waiting lists, more crimes solved or prevented, and the rest) . . .'

Insofar as it refers to education, health and other welfare services (rather than police), this is simply an unproven claim that has no support from economic analysis, British social history, or common sense. The implication is that if government spent less on welfare, parents would allow their children to wander unschooled, neglect their health, let them live in slums, stop saving for retirement or for a rainy day of sickness or unemployment. The hypothesis is a myth. The British people were educating their children, insuring for ill-health, old age and other contingencies at much lower levels of income than now and long before the state stepped in to do it for them and ended by discouraging them from doing it for themselves. The experience of other countries is that the people would now be spending more on education, health care and insurance for other eventualities voluntarily than they are now doing compulsorily. And our surveys confirm this reply to the politician by indicating that the people in all social groups, ages and political sympathies would pay for welfare privately, by prices in the market and by insurance.

EMBOURGEOISEMENT OR PROLETARIANISATION

The findings of our surveys confirm that the evidence of widening markets in luxury goods and services through the *embourgeoisement* of the 'working classes' is a more fundamental trend than the 'proletarianisation' of the middle class who have for the moment been induced by high taxes and inflation to make their peace with state education and medicine. Not least of the objections to the choice-denying universality of the Welfare State is that it obstructs the aspirations of millions of families to join the upward social mobility that a free society makes possible. Elsewhere market forces are spreading the higher standards once enjoyed only by the richest families, despite the hindrance to mobility and efficiency created by council housing, trade union restrictions, high taxation on success, subsidies for failing industry and political opposition to movement out of decaying regions with established party loyalties.

It is no paradox that Labour politicians are most conservative in resisting more radical policies that could spread choice more rapidly. Too often they put the preservation of 'working-class' culture in a captive constituency above the opportunity for individual working-class families to move into more comfortable homes, more pleasant areas and life styles where they can spend rising real incomes on still more amenities and luxuries unknown to their parents. Yet as the market offers ever-wider choice in cars, TVs, washing machines, freezers, holidays in Spain, Italy and even North America, it would be still more incongruous to combine *à la carte* in the amenities of life with *table d'hôte* in the elementals of education and medical care.

The danger for democracy is that the consent which could reasonably be claimed by government that confines itself to public goods has been progressively replaced by coercion as politicians have extended their power to supply personal, private, family benefits in education, medicine and other welfare services in which individuals could have freer choice but in which individual differences in circumstances, requirements and preferences are ignored, overlooked, or suppressed.

The Welfare State has gradually changed from the expression of compassion to an instrument of political repression unequalled in British history and in other Western industrialised societies. Representative govern-

ment which can reflect a limited range of voters' preferences for public goods has become increasingly unrepresentative government. The malignant effects for
the democratic order are intensified by its consequences
for economic management. By enlarging the sphere of
government financing to half of the national income,
the Welfare State has discouraged productive effort and
made monetary inflation and stagnating output more
difficult to correct.

Perhaps even worse, by creating expectations of
permanent secure employment in a growing bureaucracy, national and local, post-war British governments
of both major parties have created an obstacle to reform
that may endanger social peace before it is overcome.
And the longer reform is resisted, the more disruptive
it will ultimately prove to be. The inevitable disturbance
of vested interests from which politicians now shrink
can only be intensified by further delay in arresting and
reversing the drift of unlimited government towards
unlimited disaster.

The Questionnaire

	JOB NO.			DATE	CARD NO.	CLASSIFICATION DATA (CONFIDENTIAL)	SAMPLING POINT NUMBER				
(1)	(2)	(3)	(4)	JULY 1978	(9)		(10)	(11)	(12)	(13)	(14)
1	5	3	1		1						

NAME AND HOME ADDRESS (BLOCK CAPITALS)

Mr/Mrs/Miss: _____
       Initials / Surname

   ADDRESS: _____

_____

PLACE OF INTERVIEW: Home   1   Street   2   Work   3   Elsewhere   4

WORK ADDRESS: _____
(If interviewed there)

SEX:		(15)	OCCUPATION OF RESPONDENT:
	Male	1	
	Female	2	OCCUPATION OF H.O.H:
MARITAL STATUS:	Married	3	
	Single	4	
	Widowed/Separated/Divorced	5	OCCUPATION OF C.W.E. (IF APPLICABLE):
AGE GROUP:	16-24	6	
AGE LAST BIRTHDAY	25-34	7	
	35-44	8	
_____ (write in 'E'	45-54	9	COMPLETE BELOW FOR H.O.H./C.W.E:
if age group	55-64	0	Qualifications (Degrees/Apprenticeships):
estimated)	65+	X	

HOUSEHOLD COMPOSITION:		(16)	NUMBER IN H/H	
(Ring code(s)	NO CHILDREN 0-15	1		
for presence of children	CHILDREN 0-4	2		Industry/Type Of Firm:
and write in number)	5-9	3		
	10-15	4		

TOTAL CHILDREN IN HOUSEHOLD   Number Of Staff Responsible For: _____

TOTAL ADULTS (16+) IN HOUSEHOLD

TOTAL IN HOUSEHOLD   (17)   LENGTH OF INTERVIEW: _____

DECLARATION: I declare that the respondent was unknown to me before the interview took place and that this questionnaire has been conducted according to instructions and has been checked.

WOMEN ONLY:		(18)
Are you yourself responsible for the catering in your household ?	YES (housewife)	1
	NO (not housewife)	2

SIGNATURE: _____

INTERVIEWER'S NUMBER: _____

WOMEN ONLY - WORKING STATUS:	
Full-Time (30+ hours)	3
Part-Time (8-29 hours)	4
Not Working	5

DATE OF INTERVIEW: _____

This questionnaire is the property of:

OCCUPATIONAL GROUPING:		
(Classify after obtaining information opposite)	AB	6
	C1	7
	C2	8
	DE	9

England, Grosse + Associates Ltd.,
c/o PEGASUS RESEARCH LIMITED,
21 Buckingham Palace Road,
London SW1W OPP.

207

Q.1.	**ALL CONTACTS:** I'm from Pegasus Research Ltd., a market research company, and we are carrying out a survey on a number of different general sub- jects. First of all, I would like you to imagine that you had been given £2000. You have to use it all and you have a choice of six ways in which to use it. You can use it all in one way or spread it between them. Listed on this card (SHOW CARD A) are the six choices. Will you look at it and tell me how you would use this £2000 ?	HOLIDAYS ABROAD ☐ IMPROVEMENT FOR THE HOME ☐ EDUCATION FOR YOUR CHILDREN ☐ SAVING AGAINST ILL HEALTH FOR TREATMENT AND INCOME ☐ SAVING FOR RETIREMENT ☐ A CAR ☐

(20)   ROUTE

Q.2

Q.2. Most of the other questions are about the things for which the
BLUE government raises taxes from you.   I have here seven cards.
CARDS On each is something on which government and the local authorities
spend money.   I'd like you just to sort through them so you can
put at the top the item on which most money is spent, and then the
next and so on.

		NAMED 1ST (i.e. most money spent)	NAMED 2ND	NAMED 3RD	NAMED 4TH	NAMED 5TH	NAMED 6TH	NAMED 7TH
DEFENCE	(21)	1	2	3	4	5	6	7
EDUCATION	(22)	1	2	3	4	5	6	7
HEALTH	(23)	1	2	3	4	5	6	7
ROADS	(24)	1	2	3	4	5	6	7
HOUSING	(25)	1	2	3	4	5	6	7
UNEMPLOYMENT BENEFIT	(26)	1	2	3	4	5	6	7
RETIREMENT PENSIONS	(27)	1	2	3	4	5	6	7

Q.3

Note: the wording on the cards shown to respondents is reproduced on pp. 216-17.

- 2 -

Q.3.	TO ALL:	ROUTE

That's fine. Now I'd like you to try and tell me, out of each £100 that the government spends on all these seven things, how much they spend on ..... (NAME ITEM NAMED FIRST IN Q.2) Not many people know exactly but just have a guess. And what about ..... ? (NAME ITEM NAMED 2ND IN Q.2. REPEAT FOR ALL — WRITE IN SUGGESTED AMOUNT SPENT IN EVERY £100 IN THE APPROPRIATE BOX BUT REMEMBER THAT RESPONDENTS WILL NOT NECESSARILY BE ANSWERING IN THE ORDER LISTED)

OFFICE USE ONLY

			(28)	(29)	
DEFENCE					
EDUCATION			(30)	(31)	
HEALTH			(32)	(33)	
ROADS			(34)	(35)	
HOUSING			(36)	(37)	
UNEMPLOYMENT BENEFIT			(38)	(39)	
RETIREMENT PENSION			(40)	(41)	Q.4a

Q.4a. On this card (SHOW CARD B) are these same benefits. But now we've written on them the actual proportion of every £100 that the government does spend on them. Are there any which you think should have more spent on them, assuming that this means that less has to be spent on some of the others ?

		(42)	
	YES	1	Q.4b
	NO	2	Q.5
	(DON'T KNOW)	3	

Q.4b. IF 'YES' — ASK FOR EACH:
About how much more in every £100 do you think should be spent on .... ? And from which of the others do you think that this money should come ?

	HOW MUCH MORE SPENT	WRITE IN HERE WHERE COMES FROM	OFFICE USE ONLY		
			(43)	(44)	(45)
DEFENCE					
EDUCATION			(46)	(47)	(48)
HEALTH			(49)	(50)	(51)
ROADS			(52)	(53)	(54)
HOUSING			(55)	(56)	(57)
UNEMPLOYMENT BENEFIT			(58)	(59)	(60)
RETIREMENT PENSION			(61)	(62)	(63) Q.5

- 3 -

		ROUTE
Q.5a.	TO ALL Now I'd like to ask the same sort of questions again but this time the list only concerns one area very close to most people – education. On these four cards are four kinds of edu- cation. Would you tell me which you think has most spent on it by government and local authorities, next most and so on.	

Q.5b.
GREEN
CARDS — And again, at a guess, out of each £100 that the government spends
on all these four things, how much they spend on each.   Again, not
many know exactly but have a guess.   How much of every £100 do you
think they spend on nursery education ? Primary ? etc.

HOW MUCH (RANK ORDER) SPENT

	Most	Next	3rd	4th	HOW MUCH (IN EVERY £100)	OFFICE USE ONLY		
NURSERY	(64) 1	2	3	4		(68)	(69)	
PRIMARY	(65) 1	2	3	4		(70)	(71)	
SECONDARY	(66) 1	2	3	4		(72)	(73)	
HIGHER	(67) 1	2·	3	4		(74)	(75)	Q.6a

Q.6a.	On this card (SHOW CARD C) are these same areas. But now we've written on them the actual pro- portion of every £100 that the government does spend on them. Are there things that should have more spent on them, assuming that this means that less has to be spent on some of the others ?			(76)
			YES	1	Q.6b
			NO	2	Q.7
		(DON'T KNOW)	3	

Q.6b. IF 'YES' – ASK FOR EACH:
About how much more in every £100 do you think should be spent
on ...... ?

Q.6c. And from which of the others do you think that this money
should come from ?

HOW MUCH MORE SPENT	HOW MUCH (IN EVERY £100)	OFFICE USE ONLY		
		CARD 2		
NURSERY		(20)	(21)	(22)
PRIMARY		(23)	(24)	(25)
SECONDARY		(26)	(27)	(28)
HIGHER		(29)	(30)	(31)	Q.7

Q.7.	TO ALL: IF ANY ITEMS HAVE BEEN MEN- TIONED IN Q.6 FOR MORE TO BE SPENT ON THEM: You said that more should be spent on ..... (and .....). One way of making this possible, as we've suggested, is to spend less on others. But we could also collect more from taxpayers. Would you personally be prepared to pay more taxes so that more money could be spent in this way ?			(32)
			YES	1	
			NO	2	
		(DON'T KNOW)	3	Q.8

- 4 -

			ROUTE
Q.8a.	<u>TO ALL:</u> On these next four cards are kinds of payments which are made on health. Would you tell me which you think has most spent on it by the government and local authorities, which next most and so on ?		

Q.8b. And again at a guess, out of each £100 that the government spends on
YELLOW all these four things, how much do they spend on each ? How much of
CARDS every £100 they spend on the four together do you think they spend
on ..... (ITEM NAMED AS MOST AT Q.8a) And what about ...... (ITEM
NAMED AS NEXT MOST AT Q.8a. CONTINUE FOR ALL FOUR)

HOW MUCH (RANK ORDER) SPENT

	Most	Next	3rd	4th	HOW MUCH (IN EVERY £100)	OFFICE USE ONLY		
HOSPITALS	(33) 1	2	3	4		(37)	(38)	
LOCAL DOCTORS	(34) 1	2	3	4		(39)	(40)	
PRESCRIPTIONS	(35) 1	2	3	4		(41)	(42)	
PUBLIC HEALTH	(36) 1	2	3	4		(43)	(44)	Q.9a

Q.9a.	On this card (SHOW CARD D) are these same areas. But now we've written on them the <u>actual</u> pro- portion of every £100 that the government does spend on them. Are there things that should have more spent on them, assuming that this means that less has to be spent on some of the others ?		(45)
		YES	1	Q.9b
		NO	2	Q.10
		(DON'T KNOW)	3	

Q.9b. IF 'YES' - ASK FOR EACH:
About how much more in every £100 do you think should be spent
on .... ?

Q.9c. And from which of the others do you think that this money
should come ?

	HOW MUCH MORE SPENT	HOW MUCH (IN EVERY £100)	OFFICE USE ONLY			
HOSPITALS			(46)	(47)	(48)	
LOCAL DOCTORS			(49)	(50)	(51)	
PRESCRIPTIONS			(52)	(53)	(54)	
PUBLIC HEALTH			(55)	(56)	(57)	Q.10

Q.10.	<u>TO ALL:</u> IF ANY ITEMS HAVE BEEN MENTIONED IN Q.9 FOR MORE TO BE SPENT ON THEM: You said that more should be spent on ...... (and .....). One way of making this possible, as we've suggested, is to spend less on others. But we could also collect more from taxpayers. Would you personally be prepared to pay more taxes so that more money could be spent in this way ?		(58)
		YES	1
		NO	2
		(DON'T KNOW)	3	**Q.11a**

			ROUTE
Q.11a. TO ALL: So far we've talked about saving on other parts of the Health Service to provide for these facilities or spending more on higher taxes. Are there any other ways in which you think the money could be obtained by the government ?		(59)	
	YES	1	Q.11b
	NO	2	Q.12a
	OTHER ANSWER	3	

Q.11b. IF 'YES' AT Q.11a:
What are they then ?

(60)

Q.12a

Q.12a. TO ALL - SHOW CARD E:
On this card are three ways in which you personally can make use of the National Health Service. Can you tell me for each the actual cost, on average ?

OFFICE USE ONLY

		(61) (62)	
DOCTOR		(61) (62)	
PRESCRIPTION		(63) (64)	
HOSPITAL		(65) (66)	Q.12b

Q.12b. The real costs are on this card
(SHOW CARD F). Are there any
which you think it would be a
good idea if people were asked
to pay more towards than they
do now ?

	(67)
YES	1
NO	2
OTHER ANSWER	3

IF 'YES': What are they ? About how much more do you think
they ought to pay ?

	PAY MORE TO (68)	HOW MUCH MORE		
DOCTOR	1		(69) (70)	
PRESCRIPTION	2		(71) (72)	
HOSPITAL	3		(73) (74)	Q.12c

Q.12c. TO ALL:
And are there any which you think it
would be better if you could pay less
towards - if necessary having to find
your own way of meeting the costs ?

	(75)
NONE	1
DOCTOR	2
PRESCRIPTION	3
HOSPITAL	4
OTHER ANSWER	5
	(76)

IF 'YES': What are they ?

Q.13a

- 6 -

		CARD 3	
		(20)	ROUTE
Q.13a.	TO ALL: This question is about some of the things provided by your local authority rather	NONE	1	Q.13c
	than by central government. On this card (SHOW CARD G) are four ways in	LIBRARIES	2	
	which the local government spends money	SCHOOL MEALS	3	Q.13b
	and the approximate amount each costs each adult per year. Are there any	LOCAL SPORTS	4	
	of these which you think the local authorities ought to spend less on ? IF 'YES': What are they ?	POLICE	5	
Q.13b.	IF 'YES' TO Q.13a: And do you think the saving ought to		(21)	
	go to lower rates and taxes, or to go to	LOWER RATES	1	
	spending more elsewhere ?	MORE ELSEWHERE	2	
		(DON'T KNOW)	3	
		OTHER ANSWER	4	Q.13c
Q.13c.	TO ALL - SHOW CARD G AGAIN: And are there any of these which you		(22)	
	think the local authorities ought to	NONE	1	Q.14a
	spend more on ?	LIBRARIES	2	
	IF 'YES': What are they ?	SCHOOL MEALS	3	Q.13d
		LOCAL SPORTS	4·	
		POLICE	5	
Q.13d.	IF 'YES' TO Q.13c: And do you think the extra should		(23)	
	come from higher rates and taxes or	HIGHER RATES	1	
	by spending less elsewhere - either	LESS ELSEWHERE	2	
	something on this list or something else ?	(DON'T KNOW)	3	
		OTHER ANSWER	4	Q.14
Q.14.	TO ALL: Have you any children yourself ?	RECORD NUMBER	(24)	
		RECORD NUMBER AGED UNDER 19	(25)	
	And for how many of these have you paid, or planned to pay, some form of school fees at some time in their career before the age of 16 ?	RECORD NUMBER	(26)	Q.15

- 7 -

Q.15.	TO ALL - SHOW CARD H: On this card there are three possible policies which the government could adopt. Which one of them would you prefer for better or increased education ?	STATE SHOULD TAKE MORE STATE SHOULD TAKE LESS STARE SHOULD CONTINUE (DON'T KNOW)	(27) 1 2 3 4	ROUTE Q.16
Q.16.	ASK ONLY THOSE WITH CHILDREN AGED 19 OR UNDER - SEE Q.14: If the state gave you £150 a year for each child aged 11 or more which could only be spent on secondary education - and you would probably have to pay another £300 yourself to make up the fees - do you think that you would accept that offer or not ?	YES .NO (DON'T KNOW)	(28) 1 2 3	Q.17
Q.17.	And what if the offer was £300 so that you might have to add only another £150, do you think that you would accept that offer or not ?	YES NO (DON'T KNOW)	(29) 1 2 3	Q.18a
Q.18a.	TO ALL: I'd like to ask you some similar questions about the National Health Service. First of all, are you a member of any type of private health insurance which covers you for things like private hospital treatment, specialist fees and medicine ?	YES NO (DON'T KNOW)	(30) 1 2 3	Q.18b Q.19
Q.18b.	IF 'YES', GET DETAILS OF NAME OF SCHEME:			
Q.19.	TO ALL: I'd like to show you a card we used before again (SHOW CARD H AGAIN). Which of these three possible policies would you prefer for better or increased health services ?	STATE SHOULD TAKE MORE STATE SHOULD TAKE LESS STATE SHOULD CONTINUE (DON'T KNOW)	(31) 1 2 3 4	Q.20
Q.20a.	If the state gave you £30 per year for each member of your household which could only be spent on health and private health insurance provided you paid another £30 yourself, do you think that you would accept this offer or not ?	YES NO (DON'T KNOW)	(32) 1 2 3	Q.20b
Q.20b.	And what if they offered you £40 a year in this way if you added another £20 yourself ? Do you think that you would use this offer or not ?	YES NO (DON'T KNOW)	(33) 1 2 3	Q.21

	Agree Strongly	Agree	Neither Agree Nor Disagree	Disagree	Disagree Strongly		ROUTE
Q.21. **TO ALL:** Now I'm going to read you out some statements and I'd like to ask you, for each, which of the statements on this card (<u>SHOW CARD I</u>) comes nearest to your own point of view.							
PEOPLE WHO WANT TO SHOULD NOT BE ALLOWED TO PAY EXTRA TO SEND THEIR CHILDREN TO FEE-PAYING SCHOOLS	(34) 1	2	3	4	5		
PEOPLE WHO WANT TO SHOULD NOT BE ALLOWED TO PAY EXTRA FOR THEMSELVES FOR THE HEALTH SERVICES WHICH THEY NEED OUTSIDE THE HEALTH SERVICE	6	7	8	9	0		
IF I COULD GET BETTER WELFARE SERVICES I WOULD BE PREPARED TO PAY MORE FOR THEM IN HIGHER TAXES	(35) 1	2	3	4	5		
I WOULD PREFER TO HAVE A SYSTEM OF LOWER TAXES AND PAY FOR SOME WELFARE SERVICES MYSELF	6	7	8	9	0		
IN BRITAIN AS IN CALIFORNIA RECENTLY WE SHOULD BE ALLOWED TO VOTE FOR A LIMIT ON GOVERNMENT EXPENDITURE	(36) 1	2	3	4	5		Q.22

			ROUTE
Q.22. Finally, a very few simple questions about yourself. Could you tell me whether you have bought, or are in the process of buying, your house ?	YES NO OTHER (Write In)	(37) 1 2 3	
IF BOUGHT/BUYING: And could you tell me its rateable value or roughly how much you pay in rates each year ?	WRITE IN:		Q.23
Q.23. And very roughly, what proportion of your income goes in tax ? Would you say it was less than 10p. in the £, or between 10p. and 20p., or more than that ?	LESS THAN 10p. 10-20p. OVER 20p. (DON'T KNOW)	(38) 1 2 3 4	Q.24
Q.24. And which party are you most likely to vote for at the next General Election ?	CONSERVATIVE LABOUR OTHER (DON'T KNOW)	(39) 1 2 3 4	Q.25
Q.25. And at what age did you give up full time education ?	WRITE IN: _____	(40)	
Q.26. In California recently two people out of three voted to reduce taxation and accept fewer services. If there was a vote in this country on the same issue, would you vote for or against ?	WOULD VOTE FOR WOULD VOTE AGAINST	(41) 1 2	

Cards shown to respondents during interview

Question 1

Card A   *(Order rotated)*
A car
Saving for retirement
Saving against ill health for treatment and income
Education for your children
Improvement for the home
Holidays abroad

Question 4a

Card B   In every £100 spent on these seven this much is spent on:

	£
Defence	18
Education	24
Health	17
Roads	2
Housing	15
Unemployment benefit	2
Retirement pension	22
	£100

Question 6a

Card C   In every £100 spent on these four this much is spent on:

	£
Nursery schools	6
Primary schools	31
Secondary schools	50
Higher education	13
	£100

Question 9a

Card D   In every £100 spent on these four, this much is spent on:

	£
Hospitals	64
Local doctors	14
Prescriptions	11
Public Health	11
	£100

Question 12a

Card E

> A single visit to the doctor
> A single prescription
> A stay in a general hospital for a week

Question 12b

Card F

A single visit to the doctor	£4
A single prescription	£1·50
A stay in a general hospital for a week	£250

Question 13a

Card G

Libraries, museums, art galleries	£5 per adult per year
School meals and milk	£10 ,, ,, ,, ,,
Local sports and recreation facilities	£5 ,, ,, ,, ,,
Police	£25 ,, ,, ,, ,,

Questions 15 & 19

Card H

The State should take less in taxes, rates and contributions and so on to provide services *only* for people in need and leave others to pay or insure privately

The State should take more in taxes, rates and contributions and so on to pay for better or increased services which everyone would have

The State should continue the present service but allow people to contract out, pay less contributions and so on and use the money to pay for their own services

Question 21

Card I

> Agree strongly
> Agree
> Neither agree nor disagree
> Disagree
> Disagree strongly

Questionnaire for 'Proposition 13, GB'

Q1. Do you think that it would be a good idea or not such a good idea if we in Britain, as in California recently, had a referendum or special vote on reducing taxation to a maximum proportion or limit?

Good idea 1

Not such a good idea 2

Don't know 3

Q2. If there were such a referendum would you vote for or against such a maximum proportion or limit?

For 1

Against 2

Don't know 3

Would not vote...4

Q3. If there were such a referendum would you vote for or against such a maximum proportion or limit even if, as a result, Government might cut some services?

For 1

Against 2

Don't know 3

Would not vote...4

The Main Survey

The survey was designed as part of the series begun in 1963 and continued in 1965 and 1970. The field work in 1978 was directed by the principals of England, Grosse + Associates Ltd., who (originally at Mass Observation) had conducted all the earlier surveys for the IEA.

The survey repeated the key questions on attitudes to and preferences in welfare services, except for those on pensions. A high degree of continuity with the three earlier surveys was therefore obtained. In addition, new questions designed to elicit attitudes to paying for welfare by taxation and on the use of tax revenue by government were asked for the first time in 1978. The questions were, as before, constructed with the expert advice of Mr Leonard England. (The Questionnaire is reproduced at Appendix A.)

The survey was conducted in the summer of 1978, with interviewing between 14 July and 8 August in representative parts of the country (listed below).

THE SAMPLE

As in previous surveys, the sampling method chosen was quota sampling. The margins of error of quota samples are usually considered to be twice as large as those of a random sample (note on 'Sampling Error and the Results of the Survey' at Appendix D). These margins of error are considered to be acceptable for the main purpose of these surveys: to discover broad orders of magnitude and to make comparisons of the trend of results over a 15-year period.

The 1978 sample for the first time included a full complement of women of working age. It was therefore fully representative of men and women of working age (16 to 64) in Great Britain. Pensioners were again excluded for reasons discussed in the main text (Chapter 5, p. 90). Quotas were imposed within three age-groups and three occupational groups.

Details of the quotas set and the sample achieved are:

Base	Quota aimed at 2,000	Sample achieved 1,992
	%	%
Men	57	57·3
Women	43	42·7
Age		
16-34	41·4	41·4
35-54	42·4	42·0
55+	16·2	16·4
Not stated		0·2
Occupational group		
ABC1	37·4	39·3
C2	31·3	31·0
DE	31·3	29·7

There is a statistical comparison of the samples of men and women for variations in one characteristic (proportion saying they had no children under 19 years of age) in Appendix D.

COMPOSITION BY OCCUPATIONAL GROUP

Occupational (or socio-economic) groups are defined as:
AB ('Upper middle class, middle class'):
homes where the head of the household is likely to be a doctor, accountant, company director, headmaster, bank manager, etc.
C1 ('Lower middle class'):
the head of the household of this group might be a

teacher, junior civil servant, draughtsman, commercial traveller, police sergeant.

C2   ('Skilled working class'):
    foremen, carpenters, compositors and skilled workers generally.

DE   ('Working class'):
    unskilled and semi-skilled manual workers, shop assistants (and old-age pensioners).

The decision to exclude pensioners reduced the proportion of DEs in the sample compared with a random sample of all age groups because most pensioners are in the DE group, and slightly raised the proportions of the other groups, but by no more than a percentage point or two.

GEOGRAPHICAL DISTRIBUTION OF THE SAMPLE

Interviewing took place in the following 75 areas:

North	*North West*	*Yorkshire & Humberside*	*W. Midlands*
Stockton	Cumberland	Doncaster	Coventry
Darlington	Salford	Leeds	Wolverhampton
Castle Morpeth	Wirral	Bradford	Birmingham
	Liverpool	Sheffield	Nuneaton
		Hull S.E.	Wychavon
		Selby	Cannock Chase
			Warwick
E. Midlands	*East Anglia*	*South West*	*South East*
Leicester	Suffolk	Cheltenham	Slough
Blaby	Coastal	Bristol	W. Oxon
Newby	W. Norfolk	Woodspring	Brentwood
N.E. Derby		Newton	S. Oxon
Long Eaton		Abbott	Welwyn &
Northampton		W. Dorset	Hatfield
		W. Wilts.	Dacorum
		Salisbury	N. Herts.
		Weston-	Tendring
		Super-	Luton
		Mare	Portsmouth
			Southampton
			Camberley

Greater London	Wales	Scotland
Hillingdon	Swansea	W. Lothian
Bexley	Pencoed	Glasgow
Barnet	Carmarthen	Castle Douglass
Enfield		E. Lothian
Richmond		Aberdeen
Barking		Stewarty
Lambeth		Edinburgh
Hounslow		
Kingston		
Southwark		
Havering		

Distribution of the Sample by Region

	%		%
North	6	E. Anglia	3
N. West	12	S. West	8
Yorkshire &		S. East	19
Humberside	9	Gtr. London	13
W. Midlands	9	Wales	5
E. Midlands	7	Scotland	9

BASIC INFRASTRUCTURE OF THE SAMPLE

Age at which full-time education ended (Q. 25)

	Total	Men	Women
	%	%	%
Up to 14	25	25	23
Up to 15	31	32	30
Up to 16	23	23	24
Over 16	21	19	21

Political party most likely to vote for at next General Election (Q. 24)

	Men	Women
	%	%
Conservative	33	35
Labour	29	24
Others/Don't know/Won't vote	37	42

Note: Percentages do not always add up to 100 due to rounding.

Marital status

	Total %	Men %	Women %
Married	76	80	71
Single	17	16	18
Widowed/Sep'd./Divorced	7	4	11

Attitude to taxation (Q. 21)

	Men %	Women %
Reduce	51	53
Keep as now	38	35
Don't know	11	12

Whether members of private health scheme (Q. 18a, b)

	Total %	Men %	Women %
Yes	13	14	11

Scheme *(% of members of private health schemes):*

	Total %	Men %	Women %
BUPA	16	14	18
Hospital Saturday Fund	16	18	11
Hospital Saving Scheme/HSA	24	23	27
Insurance company scheme	11	12	9
Occupational scheme	11	11	10
PPP	3	3	3
Others	6	8	4

Proportion of sample with children under 19 (Q. 14)

	Total %	Men %	Women %
None	51	47	56
One child	18	19	16
2 children	21	22	18
3 children	8	8	7
4 or more	3	4	2

Respondents' Intentions on Children's Education (Q. 14)

	Total %	Men %	Women %
Proportion paying (have paid/plan to pay) private school fees	11	11	10

Number of persons in household

	Total %	Men %	Women %
1 person	7	6	7
2 people	28	26	32
3 people	22	23	21
4 people	25	27	22
5 people	11	11	12
6 or more	7	7	6

Sampling Error and the Results of the Survey

by E. J. DAVIS

The Administrative Staff College, Henley

During the last 30 years a considerable body of knowledge
and experience has been built up in the use of sampling
techniques in social and market surveys. Added to this,
while the development of computers has enabled the survey
practitioner to design and use more sophisticated and
revealing methods of analysis, the development of the
pocket calculator with square-root function makes it very
simple for the serious student or the general reader to carry
out his own calculations of confidence limits at his own desk
or fireside. The purpose of this note is to help with such
calculations.

Any survey carried out on a sample of people will be
subject to sampling error because inevitably samples short
of a complete census will vary one from another. Hence in
assessing the results from a survey, or in seeking to interpret
the differences between survey results, some estimate of the
sampling errors will be needed. (Other forms of inaccuracy
afflicting surveys arising from the design of questionnaires
or the framing of questions may lead to bias and are a
separate problem. An experienced researcher will be alert
to sources of bias and will eliminate them so far as possible,
or will indicate the likely presence of bias where complete
elimination has not been feasible.)

The basis for all theoretical work on sampling errors is the simple random sample, where each member of the population being surveyed has the same chance of inclusion in the sample to be interviewed. These samples have confidence limits such that on 95% of occasions the true population percentage relating to an attribute, such as the possession of a commodity or adherence to an opinion, will lie within a range of $\pm$ twice the 'standard error' of the percentage, measured by

$$se_p = \pm \sqrt{\frac{p(100-p)}{n}}$$

where p is the percentage calculated from the survey
      n is the number of people in the survey on which the calculation of p is based.

Unfortunately simple random samples are not practicable when interviewing a human population spread over any major geographical area, and they are not used in large-scale surveys. Modifications have to be made to the process of simple random sampling, and with each modification there is a tendency for the range of error on either side of the sample of p to widen.

This survey is based on the use of quota samples, which depart in several respects from simple random sampling. The quota sample is used so widely in both market and social research that considerable efforts have been made to arrive at methods linking the expected levels of error from quota samples to those which can be calculated from the theory of simple random sampling. A major investigation, which produced results now accepted as standard, was carried out by Moser and Stuart in 1952.[1] It showed that the standard error of a quota sample properly conducted could be taken

[1] C. A. Moser and A. Stuart, 'An experimental study of quota sampling,' *Journal of the Royal Statistical Society,* CXVI, Part 4, 1953.

as being about 1·4 times that of a random sample of equivalent size.

When large national surveys are undertaken the design of the sample, whether random or quota, becomes more complex. Normally Local Authority Areas or Constituencies are selected as a first stage, and the ultimate selection of individuals for the sample is made on some form of 'cluster' basis within each of the selected first-stage areas. Such multi-stage and clustering procedures reduce the costs of surveys, but again they tend to increase the standard errors of the results above the levels expected from simple random sampling. The design of a survey will determine the specific 'design factor' which will apply to convert the standard error for simple random sampling to a value which can be used with that survey, but examination of a number of surveys for which the detailed calculations have been made indicates that a factor of about 1·4 provides a fair practical estimate.[2]

Taking both of these effects, due to the use of multi-stage clustered samples and of quota sampling, the standard error of a well-conducted quota sample is seen to be about twice the standard error of a simple random sample. Hence the figures obtained from the simple calculation shown above need to be doubled before being used as an indication of the precision of an observed percentage p, and the calculation of the 95% limits is then based on a range of four times the simple standard error, i.e., $\pm 4 \text{ se}_p$.

Where interest lies in assessing whether a difference between two sample results is significant or whether it might merely be due to chance variations between samples, the usual formula for calculating the standard error of a difference between two percentages is used. If the two percentages are denoted by p_1 and p_2, and the sizes of the two sample bases by n_1 and n_2, the formula for the

[2] C. A. Moser and G. Kalton, *Survey Methods in Social Investigation,* Heinemann, London, 1971, pp. 201-2.

standard error of the difference between the two percentages using simple random sampling is given by

$$\text{se}_d = \pm \sqrt{\frac{p_1(100-p_1)}{n_1} + \frac{p_2(100-p_2)}{n_2}} .$$

The 95% limits for quota sampling are again subject to a factor of 4 and are given by the range $\pm$ 4se$_d$. If the observed difference between the two percentages exceeds this value of four times the standard error of the difference, there is less than one chance in 20 that such a result could have arisen simply from sampling fluctuations.

The Table at the end of this Appendix shows the estimated 95% limits for quota samples related to selected values of p and of n. To calculate the 95% limits for a difference between p_1 and p_2, take the figures shown in the Table at appropriate values of p and n, square them, add the squares together, and take the square root of their sum.

Examples—assuming the use of a pocket calculator

I. Comparisons between men in 1970 and 1978

The survey of 1970 was based on a sample of 2,005 men in the working population aged between 18 and 65 years. 41% of the sample said that they had ended their full-time education at the age of 14 or under.

In the 1978 survey the sample of working men was 1,142, aged between 16 and 65. 25% said that they had ended full-time education at the aged of 14 or under.

Three questions can be put:
(i)   How precise is the figure of 41% saying 14 or under in 1970?
(ii) How precise is the 1978 figure of 25%?
(iii) Is the difference between the two figures significant, or could it have arisen merely by chance?

For the 1970 figure:
$$p = 41\%, \text{ and } (100-p) = 59\%$$
$$n = 2,005$$

Hence $se_p = \sqrt{\dfrac{41 \times 59}{2005}} = \sqrt{1 \cdot 206} = 1 \cdot 1\%.$

Allowing for the use of quota sampling, the estimated 95 % limits in 1970 are: 41 % $\pm$ 4$\times$1·1 % or 41 % $\pm$ 4$\frac{1}{2}$%

i.e., between $36\frac{1}{2}\%$ and $45\frac{1}{2}\%$.

For the 1978 figure:

$p = 25\%$ and $(100 - p) = 75\%$

$n = 1,142$

Hence $se_p = \sqrt{\dfrac{25 \times 75}{1142}} = \sqrt{1 \cdot 642} = 1 \cdot 3\%.$

Allowing for the use of quota sampling the estimated 95 % limits in 1978 are: 25%$\pm$4$\times$1·3 % or 25%$\pm$5 %

i.e., between 20 % and 30 %.

Simple inspection of the limits shows the existence of a real change as the lower limit in 1970 was $36\frac{1}{2}\%$ and the upper limit in 1978 was 30 %. However, as an example of the calculation of the 95 % limits of the difference between two percentages the following working is given:

$$se_d = \sqrt{\frac{41 \times 59}{2005} + \frac{25 \times 75}{1142}}$$

$$= \sqrt{1 \cdot 206 + 1 \cdot 642}$$

$$= \sqrt{2 \cdot 848}$$

$$= 1 \cdot 7\%.$$

Hence for quota sampling the 95 % limits of the difference between the two percentages are $\pm$ 4$\times$1·7 % = $\pm$7 %. As the observed difference is 41 % $-$25 % = 16 %, a real change appears to have occurred.

II. Comparisons between men and women in 1978

In the survey of 1978 47 % of the 1,142 men interviewed said that they had no children under 19 years of age. 56 %

of the 850 women interviewed said that they had no children under 19 years of age. Is the difference real in that the proportions of men and women in the working population with children under 19 years of age do differ; or could the difference be due to sampling fluctuations?

For the men:

$$p = 47\% \text{ and } (100 - p) = 53\%$$
$$n = 1,142$$

Hence $se_p = \sqrt{\dfrac{47 \times 53}{1142}} = \sqrt{2 \cdot 181} = 1 \cdot 5\%.$

Allowing for the use of quota sampling, the estimated 95% limits for men are $47\% \pm 4 \times 1 \cdot 5\%$ or $47\% \pm 6\%$

i.e., *between 41% and 53%.*

For the women:

$$p = 56\% \text{ and } (100 - p) = 44\%$$
$$n = 850$$

Hence $se_p = \sqrt{\dfrac{56 \times 44}{850}} = \sqrt{2 \cdot 899} = 1 \cdot 7\%.$

Allowing for the use of quota sampling, the estimated 95% limits for women are $56\% \pm 4 \times 1 \cdot 7\%$ or $56\% \pm 7\%$

i.e., *between 49% and 63%.*

In this case inspection shows that the figure for men could be as high as 53%, while that for women could be as low as 49%. However these are independent limits, and there is only a very small probability that each of these figures would be at its limit at the same time. Hence it is necessary to calculate the standard error of the difference, which takes account of the joint probabilities in the situation. The calculation is as follows:

$$se_d = \sqrt{\dfrac{47 \times 53}{1142} + \dfrac{56 \times 44}{850}}$$

$$= \sqrt{2 \cdot 181 + 2 \cdot 899}$$

$$= \sqrt{5 \cdot 080}$$

$$= 2 \cdot 25.$$

Hence for quota sampling the 95% limits of the difference between the percentages of men and women in the working population who have no children under 19 years of age are $\pm 4 \times 2 \cdot 25 = \pm 9\%$.

The difference between the percentages for men and women is 9%. This puts the probability that the observed difference has arisen simply by chance at only 1 in 20, indicating that it is almost certain that a real difference is indicated between the proportions of men and women in the working population who have children under 19 years of age.

Unless differences between groups are very wide, it is not sufficient when making comparisons to look only at the separate 95% limits and the extent to which they might overlap. The observed difference needs to be compared with the standard error of the difference if a proper interpretation is to be made.

Sample size n	Percentage p; or (100 − p)					
	10	15	20	30	40	50
100	12	14	16	18	20	20
150	10	12	13	15	16	16
200	8½	10	11	13	14	14
400	6	7	8	9	10	10
600	5	6	6½	7½	8	8
850	4	5	5½	6	7	7
1000	4	4½	5	6	6	6
1142	3½	4	5	5½	6	6
1400	3	4	4	5	5	5
1600	3	3½	4	4½	5	5
2005	3	3	3½	4	4½	4½

Addresses of Sources of Information
on Private Supply of Alternatives to the State

(a) EDUCATION

Independent Schools Information Service
26 Caxton Street,
London, S.W.1.

Association for Independent Education
Avalon, Mill Lane,
Horndon-on-the-Hill,
Stanford-le-Hope, Essex.

Education Otherwise
Lower Shaw Farm House,
Shaw, Swindon,
Wiltshire.

(b) MEDICINE

BUPA   British United Provident Association,
        Provident House,
        Essex Street,
        London WC2R 3AX.

PPP   Private Patients Plan,
        Eynsham House,
        Crescent Road,
        Tunbridge Wells,
        Kent TN1 2PL.

WPA   Western Provident Association,
Culver House,
Culver Street,
Bristol BS1 5JE.

EHAS   Exeter Hospital Aid Society,
5 & 7 Palace Gate,
Exeter EX1 1UE.

CSMAA Civil Service Medical Aid Association,
Charles House,
Kensignton High Street,
London W14 8QL.

BCWA   Bristol Contributary Welfare Association,
25 Victoria Street,
Bristol BS1 6AB.

PHSA   Provincial Hospital Services Association,
44 Harpur Street,
Bedford MK40 2QU.

MSHCA Mid Southern Hospital Contributory Association,
29 Castle Street,
Reading RG1 7SL

PPA   Private Patients (Anglia) Ltd.,
124 Thorpe Road,
Norwich NR1 1RS.

RPA   Revenue Provident Association,
New Wing,
Somerset House,
London WC2R 1LB.

HPIS   Hospital Plan Insurance Services,
44 Baker Street,
London W1E 2EZ.

HSA   Hospital Saving Association,
        30 Lancaster Gate,
        London W2 3LT.

AMA   Allied Medical Assurance,
        Trafalgar House,
        11 Waterloo Place,
        London SW1

AMI   American Medical International
        4 Cornwall Terrace,
        London NW1 4QB.

IEA Studies on the Economics of British Social Policy

Since its inception in 1957 the Institute has devoted some one-third of its work to studies of the conditions of the supply of and the demand for 'welfare'—education, medical care, housing, pensions, and the maintenance of income. Its emphasis on these subjects is derived from the view that welfare policy is under-estimated in public discussion although it accounts for a half of public finance, that the economic aspects of social policy are not given sufficient weight by non-economists, and that economists interested in the working and development of markets in welfare have given more attention to the conditions of supply, e.g. the degree of competition, than to the conditions of demand, especially the distribution of income and its supplementation or provision by the state to people who do not generate sufficient earnings to pay market prices.

This note summarises the studies published by the Institute in the last 22 years. Authors are described by their present or latest appointments except where otherwise stated.

1957 *Pensions in a Free Society*

Seldon, A., Editorial Director, IEA.

A critique of the Labour party's proposals for national superannuation evolved by R. H. S. Crossman advised by Professors B. Abel-Smith, R. M. Titmuss, and P. Townsend.

235

1960   *To Let:* HP 2[1]

   Macrae, N., Deputy Editor of *The Economist.*

   An examination of the development of rent restriction and its effects in inhibiting the supply of housing to let.

   Pensions for Prosperity: HP 4

   Seldon, A.

   A critique of the Conservative proposals for graduated state pensions evolved by Mr J. Boyd-Carpenter, then Minister of Pensions.

1961   *Health Through Choice:* HP 14

   Lees, D. S., Professor of Industrial Economics, University of Nottingham.

   A pioneering analysis of the economics of the National Health Service.

1962   *Libraries: Free-for-All?:* HP 19

   Herbert, A. P., Harris, R., General Director, IEA.

   A study of the financing of public libraries and of the case for an annual charge (Herbert) and a charge per borrowing (Harris).

1963   *Relief for Ratepayers:* HP 20

   Ilersic, A. R., Professor of Social Studies, Bedford College, University of London.

   A study of the financing of local authority services, concluding with the case for, and the yield of, charges for housing, education, and others.

[1] HP Hobart Paper   RM Research Monograph
   OP Occasional Paper RPE Readings in Political Economy
   EP Eaton Paper   RR Research Report

1963 *Choice in Welfare 1963:* RR

Harris, R., Seldon, A.

The first examination of public knowledge and preferences in education, medical care and pensions based on
a field survey with priced alternatives.

1964 *Monopoly or Choice in Health Services?:* OP 3

Jewkes, J., formerly Professor of Industrial Organisation,
University of Oxford, Jewkes, S., Kemp, A., Professor
of Economics, Claremont College, California, Lees, D. S.

A critique of the sociologists' case for universal state
medical services financed by taxation.

Education for Democrats: HP 25 (Reprinted 1970)

Peacock, A. T., Principal-Designate and Professor of
Economics, University College at Buckingham, and
Wiseman, J., Professor of Applied Economics and
Director of the Institute of Social and Economic Research,
University of York.

A study of the financing of state education and of the
arguments for state grants, loans and vouchers.

Taxmanship: HP 26 (2nd edition 1970)

Clark, C., Research Fellow, Monash University,
Australia.

An inquiry into the relationship between taxes and prices
and into the case for financing welfare services by methods
other than taxes.

Land in the Market: HP 30

Denman, D., Professor of Land Economics and Head of
Department, University of Cambridge.

A study of the institutional framework of land ownership
and its implications, *inter alia*, for housing policy.

238   OVER-RULED ON WELFARE

1965   *Education and the State* (Second edition 1970)

West, E. G., Professor of Economics, Carleton University, Ottawa.

A re-examination of the history and evolution of British state education since 1870.

The Inconsistencies of the National Health Service: OP 7

Buchanan, J. M., Professor of Economics and Director of the Centre for Study of Public Choice at Virginia Polytechnic Institute, Blacksburg, Virginia.

A comparative study of taxation and market financing of medical care.

Choice in Welfare 1965: RR

Harris, R., and Seldon, A.

The second examination of public knowledge and preferences in education, medical care, and pensions based on a field survey with priced alternatives.

1966   *Financing University Education:* OP 12

Prest, A. R., Professor of Economics with special reference to the Public Sector, University of London, at the London School of Economics.

A study of the economics of loans for university students.

Cost-Benefit Analysis and Public Expenditure: EP 8

(Third edition, Second Impression 1974)

Peters, G. H., Brunner Professor of Economic Science and Head of Department, University of Liverpool.

A critique of the notion of cost-benefit analysis and its implications for welfare (and other government) policies.

Economic Consequences of the Professions: RM 2

Lees, D. S.

An investigation into the supply of medical (and other) professions with special reference to the avoidance of monopoly.

1967 *Paying for the Social Services:* OP 16 (Second edition 1968)

Houghton, D. (Lord), former Minister for Social Services, 1964-67.

A re-consideration of the financing of state welfare with a statement of the case for shifting emphasis from taxation to social insurance and for introducing hospital charges and taxing sickness benefits.

Towards a Welfare Society: OP 13

Alexander, A., writer, Carmichael, J., independent economist, Clark, C., Harris, R., Hutton, G., independent economist, Ilersic, A. R., Lees, D. S., Murley, R. S., President of the Royal College of Surgeons, Peacock, A. T., Pennance, F. G., Seale, J., physician, Seldon., A. Welch, C., Deputy Editor, *Daily Telegraph,* West, E, G.

The report of a study group for a conference of the British National Conference of Social Welfare (in association with the National Council of Social Service).

Housing, Town Planning and the Land Commission: HP 40

Pennance, F. G.

A critique of the rationale of the Land Commission and an argument for its abolition.

Universal or Selective Social Benefits?: RM 8

Seldon, A., Gray, H., economic adviser at the Department of the Environment.

An analytical and empirical examination of the comparative merits of universality and selectivity in state welfare.

Taxation and Welfare: RM 14

Seldon, A.

A further scrutiny of aspects of state welfare and public attitudes to means tests and alternative methods of payment.

Education: a Framework for Choice: RPE 1 (Second edition 1970)

Beales, A. C. F., Blaug, M., Professor in the Economics of Education, University of London Institute of Education, West, E. G., Veale, Sir Douglas, Boyson, R., Member of Parliament.

A collection of papers on historical and economic aspects of choice in education and its financing.

1968　*After the NHS:* OP 21

Seldon, A.

Amplified text of a Paper prepared for a Conference of voluntary health insurance organisations in Sydney, analysing the scope for the expansion of private insurance in Britain as the NHS exhibits strains accompanying growing deficiencies of tax finance.

The Price of Blood: HP 41

Cooper, M., Donald Reid Professor of Economics, University of Otago, New Zealand and Culyer, A. J., Reader in Economics at the University of York.

An examination of the methods of financing the supply of blood and the scope for paying donors and charging recipients.

Economics, Education and the Politician: HP 42 (Second impression 1976)

West, E. G.

Further analysis of the financing of education with special reference to the theories of Buchanan and Tullock on the motivation of politicians in maximising electoral returns from social policy.

Dependency and the Family: RM 16

Bremner, M., psychologist.

A discussion of the role of the family in decision making: illustrated by the findings of field research.

The Cost of Council Housing: RM 18

Gray, H.

A dissection of the economic history of council housing, and its effects and the alternatives.

Choice in Housing: RR

Pennance, F. G., Gray, H.

An application to housing of the methods developed in *Choice in Welfare,* 1963 and 1965.

1969 *Towards an Independent University:* OP 25
(Second edition 1970)

Ferns, H. S., Professor of Political Science and Head of Department, the University of Birmingham.

A statement of the case for private financing of university teaching, research and scholarship.

Economic Aspects of Student Unrest: OP 26

Peacock, A. T., Culyer, A. J.

A discussion of causes and possible cures by the development of student fees financed by loans.

Private Capital for New Towns: OP 28

Ling, A. G., formerly President of the Royal Town Planning Institute, Rouse, J., President of the Rouse Company and formerly a member of President Eisenhower's Advisory Committee on Housing, West, W. A., Professor of Law Relating to Land, Faculty of Urban and Regional Studies, University of Reading, Bowley, M., formerly Professor of Political Economy, University College, London, Lichfield, N., Professor in the Economics of Environmental Planning, University College, London, Pennance, F. G.

A report of five lectures at a conference on the development of new towns by private financing.

Housing Market Analysis and Policy: HP 48

Pennance, F. G., West, W. A.

An analysis of the economic theory of the housing market and the implications for housing policy by Pennance, with an essay on the legal framework by West.

1970   *Expansionism in Social Insurance:* OP 32

Myers, R. J., formerly Government Chief Actuary, Social Security Administration, US Department of Health, Education and Welfare, now Professor of Actuarial Science, Temple University, Philadelphia.

A revelation of the tendency of politicians and civil servants to inflate graduated social insurance to the progressive exclusion of private insurance, saving, and pensions.

Policy for Poverty: RM 20

Christopher, A., General Secretary to the Inland Revenue Staff Federation, Polanyi, G., Seldon, A., Shenfield, B., Vice-Chairman, W.R.V.S.

The report of a study group on the failure of universal social benefits to remove poverty and an examination of minimum income alternatives, concluding with a recommendation for the adoption of a reverse income tax.

Choice in Welfare 1970: RR

Harris, R., Seldon, A.

The third examination of public knowledge and preferences in education, medical care and pensions based on a field survey with priced alternatives.

Social Benefits and Tax Rates: RM 22

Prest, A. R.

A short study of implicit and explicit marginal tax rates in England and Wales.

Taxation: A Radical Approach: RPE 4

Tanzi, Vito, Associate Professor of Economics, American University, Washington, D. C., Bracewell-Milnes, J. B., Economic Consultant, Fiscal-Economic Institute, Erasmus University, Rotterdam, Myddelton, D. R., Professor of Finance and Accounting, Cranfield College of Technology.

A re-assessment of the high level of British taxation and the scope for its reduction.

1971 *Housing and the Whitehall Bulldozer:* HP 52

McKie, R., Professor of Town and Country Planning, Queens University, Belfast.

A study of the maintenance of demand and a proposal for the cellular renewal of twilight zones.

1972 *Rates or Prices?:* HP 54

Maynard, A. K., Lecturer in Economics, University of York, King, D. N., Lecturer in Economics, University of Stirling.

A study of the economics of local government and its replacement by the market.

Verdict on Rent Control: RPE 7

Hayek, F. A., Nobel Laureate 1974, Friedman, M., Nobel Laureate 1976, Stigler, G. J., Charles R. Walgreen Distinguished Service Professor of American Institutions, University of Chicago, Jouvenel, Bertrand de, Editor, *Analyse et Prevision*, Paish, F. W., Professor of Economics, London School of Economics, 1949-65, Rydenfelt, S., formerly Lecturer in Economics, University of Lund, Sweden, Pennance, F. G.

Essays on the economic consequences of political action to restrict rents in five countries.

The Long Debate on Poverty: RPE 9 (Second edition 1974)

Hartwell, R. M., Professorial Fellow, Nuffield College, Oxford, Mingay, G. E., Professor of Agrarian History, University of Kent, Boyson, R., McCord, N., Professor of History, University of Newcastle upon Tyne, Hanson, C. G., Professor of Economics, University of Newcastle upon Tyne, Coats, A. W., Professor of Economic and Social History, University of Nottingham, Chaloner, W. H., Professor of History, University of Manchester, Henderson, W. O., formerly Reader in International Economic History, University of Manchester, Jefferson, J. M., Head of Economic Development, Group Planning Division, Shell International Petroleum Company, Gash, N., Professor of History, St. Andrews University.

Essays on industrialisation and 'the condition of England'.

The Economics of Charity: RPE 12

Alchian, A., Professor of Economics, University of California, Allen, W. R., Professor of Economics, University of California, Cooper, M., Culyer, A., Ireland, M., Assistant Professor of Law, Washington University School of Law, Ireland, T., Professor of Economics, University of Missouri, Johnson, D. B., Professor of Economics, Louisiana State University, Koch, J., Professor of Economics, Illinois State University, Salsbury, A. J., Consultant Haematologist, Brompton Hospital, Tullock, Gordon.

Essays on the comparative economics and ethics of giving and selling, with application to blood.

1973   *How Much Inequality?:* RM 31

Polanyi, G., Wood, J. B., Deputy Director, IEA.

A critical inquiry into the 'evidence'.

How Much Subsidy?: RM 32

Prest, A. R.

A study of the economic concept and measurement of subsidies in the United Kingdom.

Government and the Land: RPE 13

Walters, A. A., Professor of Political Economy, Johns Hopkins University, Baltimore, Maryland, Pennance, F. G., West, W. A., Denman, D. R., Bracewell-Milnes, J. B., Denman, S. E., Fellow of the Royal Institution of Chartered Surveyors, Slough, D. G., Chairman and Managing Director, Taylor Woodrow Homes, Ingram, S., Partner, Thomas Cordiner, Cunningham & Partners.

Essays on aspects of land development, town planning and state control.

1975 *Experiment with Choice in Education:* HP 64

Maynard, A. K.

An analysis of new methods of consumer financing to bring more resources into education by vouchers and loans.

1976 *Pricing or Taxing?:* HP 71

Harris, R., Seldon, A.

Evidence on charging for local government services invited by the Layfield Committee and a critique of its Report.

The Dilemmas of Government Expenditure: RPE 15

Bacon, R., Fellow of Lincoln College and Lecturer in Econometrics, University of Oxford, Eltis, W., Fellow of Exeter College and Lecturer in Economics, University of Oxford, Wilson, T., Adam Smith Professor of Political Economy, University of Glasgow, Wiseman, J., Howell, D., Member of Parliament, Pardoe, J., Member of Parliament, Marquand, D., Professor of Contemporary

History and Politics, University of Salford, Lynn, R., Professor of Psychology, New University of Ulster.

Essays in political economy by economists and parliamentarians.

1977 *Poverty before Politics:* HP 73

Clark, C.

A proposal for a Reverse Income Tax.

Paying by Degrees: HP 75

Crew, M. A., Professor of Business Administration and Director, Business Research Centre, Rutgers University, New Jersey, Young, A., Assistant Lecturer, Paisley College of Technology.

A study of the financing of higher education by grants, loans and vouchers.

The State of Taxation: RPE 16

Prest, A. R., Clark, C., Elkan, W., Professor of Economics, University of Durham, Rowley, C. K., Professor of Economics, University of Newcastle upon Tyne, Bracewell-Milnes, J. B., Pearce, I. F., Director of Research, Econometric Model Building Unit, University of Southampton.

Essays on the UK tax system and proposals for its reform.

1979 *Over-ruled on Welfare*

Harris, R., Seldon, A.

The fourth examination of public knowledge and preferences in education and medical care based on a field survey with priced alternatives.

Index of Names

Titmuss, R. M., 6, 9, 15
Townsend, Peter, 13, 16
Treasure, J. A. P., xxix
Trzeciakowski, Witold, 81n
Tullock, Gordon, 10, 10-11n,
  171n
Tyler, Wat, 20

Wagner, R. E., 10n
Walden, Brian, 76n
Wanniski, Jude, 24n
West, E. G., xxix, 99n, 190
Williams, Shirley, 13, 16
Wiseman, Jack, 82
Wood, John B., xxix

Vaizey, Lord (John), 72

Young, Alistair, 100, 135n